Governing

The Metropolis

BOOKS BY S. GREER

Governing the Metropolis
Metropolitics: A Study
of Political Culture

Governing

The Metropolis

Scott Greer

Associate Professor of

Political Science and Sociology

Director, Center for

Metropolitan Studies

Northwestern University

John Wiley and Sons, Inc.

New York · London · Sydney

Library of Congress Catalog Card Number: 62—18353

Printed in the United States of America

Preface

In the past decade the American people have slowly become aware of a dramatic fact. We are an urban nation and the metropolis is our native habitat. Though we still think of a diffuse nation living in cities, small towns, and open-country neighborhoods, most of us will live out our lives within the compass of a few very large cities.

Little in our past has prepared us for this. Our political thought was developed from a concern with the direct democracy possible (at least in theory) within small governmental units, "governing best when governing least." Today our governments are, in sum, a vast network, corresponding to giant business corporations and great metropolitan complexes. Today we spend over sixty billion dollars a year for state and local government. The reason is clear; government grows precisely because the entire society is increasing in scale.

Concern with the federal government has sometimes led us to neglect the local community and its governance. And to be sure, war and economic prosperity, two of the great issues of the day, cannot be settled here. But other issues can and will be, and at the local level the average citizen has his major opportunity to control his collective fate. Democracy is an experiment in education; that education is most accessible in the local political community.

But the local community has changed radically with the growth of the metropolis. It cannot be understood without attention to the transformation of our entire society that produces the metropolis. For these reasons I have written this study of politics and government in our metropolitan areas. I believe that knowledge precedes commitment, and our ignorance of the political world of the metropolis accounts for much of our apathy and cynicism. I believe knowledge, even of failure, is more useful than ignorance.

This book is an effort to summarize many studies of politics and government in metropolitan areas. It rests upon the work of scores of scholars, actors, and observers. It is by no means complete. Metropolitanization has come upon us so rapidly that we are still struggling to understand it. Undoubtedly many complexities are omitted, many generalizations are debatable. I have followed the strategy of sacrificing detailed documentation to the demands of intellectual order. Thus the book is more than a photograph of big city government; it aims to be an analysis.

My reasons for maintaining this emphasis are as follows. First, I believe any student appreciates intellectual order and develops more control through understanding a clearly stated theory than through exposure to a hundred case studies. After all, his life is filled with case studies; he comes to the college for a more general understanding and the power that flows from it. Second, I believe that the collective enterprise of understanding our political communities is furthered by the presentation of clearly stated and logical theory. Even when it is not valid in all respects, it may still frame significance so that important questions can be asked.

As a citizen, I believe that the questions that can be asked of our local polities are among the most important ones we must answer. The mass society and the administrative state begin at home. They begin in the inability of local governance to shoulder the burden of decision. They are nourished through the ignorance of citizenry and local leaders alike. They terminate in the death of significance. It has been said that Americans hate politics. It has also been said that one cannot love that which he does not understand. If this book has any success, perhaps it will help us to be more realistic, informed, and tough-minded about our local polity. It is, after all, a major determinant of our common fate.   SCOTT GREER

Otis, Oregon

May, 1962

Contents

Part I   The Creation of a Metropolitan World

1   *The City in Time and Space*   *3*
   The City as a Center of Societal Order, 4
   Urbanization in the Past: The City as an Island, 6
  Increase in Scale and Societal Transformation   9
   Energy, Transportation, and the City, 10
   Some Consequences of Increase in Scale, 12
  The Changing American Urban Community   15
   Increase in Scale and the Development of the United
     States, 16
   The History of our Cities in the Light of Techno-
     logical Change, 17
   The Dispersion of the City, 20

2   *The People of the Metropolis*   *23*
   Variation of Urban Lives: Ethnicity, Social Rank, and
     Life Style, 23
   Increasing Social Choice and Variation, 28
  The Map of the Metropolis and the Division of Re-
     wards, 31
   The Inherited City and the Changing Neighbor-
     hoods, 33
  The Maintenance of Order in the Urban Community 35
   The City as a Problem of Social Order, 36
   Solutions to the Problem of Order, 37
   The Basis of Urban Order: The Local Political Com-
     munity, 39

Part II   The Governmental Response to
           Metropolitanization

3   *The Governmental Mosaic of the Metropolis*   *45*
      The Norms of Local Government in the United
        States, 46
      How the Cities Grew Up, 49
    Central City versus Suburbs   50
      Difference in People and Difference in Government, 52
      The Origins of Suburban Municipalities, 53
    The Governmental Dichotomy and Some Consequences
      55
      Some Auguries and a Question, 56

4   *The Governance of the Central City*   *59*
      Economics of Machine Government, 62
      The Power Elite of the City Today, 64
    Social Change and the Machine   65
      Corporate Merger and Local Politics, 66
      Population Change and the Machine, 68
      Growth of the Giant Bureaucracies, 69
    The Machine of the Incumbents   71
      The Disaster of Total Victory, 73
      One-Party Government and Control of the Machine, 74
    The Weakening of Positive Government   77

5   *The Suburbs: "Republics in Miniature"*   *83*
      Suburbs and Suburbs: Variations, 85
    The Ideal Suburban Polity   87
    Political Issues of Suburbia   90
      Suburban Community Problems, 91
      Problems into Political Issues, 93
    Suburban Political Orders   96
      Upward Ho!, 97
      Valhalla, 99

Part III   The Future of the Metropolity

6   *The Schizoid Polity and the Drive for Reunification 107*
     Consequences of the Dichotomy: I. The Political Process
          108
     Consequences of the Dichotomy: II. The Governmental
          Process   110
          The Problem of Providing Services, 112
          The Problem of Equity, 114
          The Problem of Consensus: What Kind of City?, 117
     The Drive for Reintegration   119
          The History of Metropolitan Government Plans, 121
          The Barriers to Change, 124

7   *The Metropolity and Its Future*   *129*
          Substitutes for Metropolitan Government, 129
          Consequences of Using Substitutes, 132
     The Future Course of the Metropolis   134
          The Changing Tasks of the Central City, 136
          The Developing Suburbs, 138
     The Future Polity   139
          Policy for the Central City, 141
          Policy for Suburbia, 144

     Index   *151*

Part I

The Creation of a
Metropolitan World

1

The City in Time
and Space

Most of human history has been made in cities. It is no accident that the word "civilization" is derived from the city, as the word "politics" is derived from the ancient Greek word for the city state, the *polis*. The centers of wealth and military power, of government and culture, have always been cities, and the human societies complex enough to have a history have been designated civilizations. It is worth while to spell out the reasons for this, since they go as deep as the city's reason for being.

The city is a settlement of human population which cannot support itself from its own soil. It can exist only by exchange of goods and services with the farmers, herdsmen, miners, fishermen, and others who gather and extract materials from the earth. Thus it is completely dependent for its livelihood upon those outside the city. (Most estimates indicate that New York City could not survive a week without imports from outside the city limits.) How, then, can a unit so dependent for its existence be said to dominate the society, and through the society, history?

3

The city has dominated through its crucial role in the division of labor of society. For the dependence is not one-way: city and countryside are interdependent, each carrying out tasks which are uneconomical, difficult, or impossible for the other. The city entered history with the neolithic era—the point in human development when man invented agriculture and the storage of grain. It was only then that city folk could live from the produce of others. They obtained this produce through plundering the country men subdued in war (this became first tribute, then taxes). They obtained it also through trade. The city, by organization of military force, became the political center and market for the total society.

To be sure, we find it difficult to see much "exchange" in the surrender of loot to an invading army. If we stand back a little, however, and look at the consequences of urban conquest and dominance, we find that even the earliest cities contributed materially to the welfare of the peasant villagers. First, they provided protection against other "outside" marauders. Second, they maintained a degree of order within their boundaries. Third, and very important, they established peaceable communication within the territories they dominated. Thus the city established the state, and the state made possible the cooperation of diverse people over space and through time. In return for regularized tribute or taxes the city created order—the famous *Pax Romana* is only one instance. Furthermore, by creating a larger social system the city made it possible for peasant villagers to avoid starvation. When crops failed they could use the exchange system of the larger society, importing grain from other regions where crops were better that year.

THE CITY AS THE CENTER OF SOCIETAL ORDER

Thus one basic export of the city is order. We see this today in the location of our governmental agencies; their headquarters are not in the open country or the small towns, but in metropolitan areas. This is equally true of the business corporations, of the major labor unions, of the churches and the universities and the communications industries—television, radio, publishing. Vast segments of human behavior throughout the United States are regulated from the control centers of cities. The market price changes in New York or Chicago, and farmers go bankrupt in California; a decision is made by the Teamsters Union and management officials, and the cost of freight goes up in an Ozark hamlet; a speech is made and a vote is taken in Washington, D.C., and all American men over the age of eighteen report to their draft boards.

The major importance of order as a product of the city is obscured for us. Our cities are not only centers of communication and control but are also workshops of the society. This task is, however, relatively new to the city. Through most of human history two conditions have limited the importance of the city as a workshop and marketplace for the whole society. First, transport was so costly and slow that all possible work was done at the place where goods were released from the earth. Second, the goods produced in the city did not differ radically from those that could be produced in the peasant villages. Consequently, the city tended to engage in "trinket trade," dealing in small objects of high value—rarities, jewels, spices—which had both individuality and low shipping costs, and could be widely traded. But the city needed tons of raw materials for the human and animal population— food, fabric, forest products and other building materials, and these could be shipped easily only by water. Thus the great cities of earlier societies were on the rivers or seacoasts. Here the heavy and vital goods from the hinterland could be transported, floated downriver or carried along the coasts. The journey upriver was slow and costly, and it was made by empty boats.

The early cities lived off tribute and trinkets; they returned little to the hinterland, except order. Their workshops produced goods for the urbanites, or goods to be exchanged with those of other cities, or a few light and costly items which became standard equipment for the more prosperous peasantry. As one consequence, the peasant villages were relatively self-sufficient; since their material needs were largely supplied locally, they could watch with equanimity the collapse of one city's empire and the rise of another. For them it meant merely a change in policemen and tax collectors. Locally self-sufficient, they produced little more than enough for local needs; they were subsistence economies.

URBANIZATION IN THE PAST: THE CITY AS AN ISLAND

As a consequence of their economies, the great societies of the past never became really urban. Though the city of Rome may have reached a population of one million at the height of the Empire, the great mass of the Empire's population (probably 90 per cent or more) lived as it had for thousands of years in peasant villages far from the coasts. While a sophisticated culture developed in the "world cities," most human beings through most of history lived in what Turner calls the "daemonic universe of the peasant village."[1] Their thought and social behavior were dominated by tradition, superstition, and fear of the unknown.

With the collapse of the Roman society the city disappeared from western Europe for many centuries. To be sure, there were small settlements—headquarters for the Church, a few depots for goods exchanged with the east. On the whole, however, the political fragmentation of the West led to such an extreme decentralization that the subsistence economy of the feudal domain became the basic

[1] Ralph Turner, *The Great Cultural Traditions,* New York: McGraw-Hill Book Company, 1941, especially Chapter XX.

unit of both political and economic life. Then slowly, on the rivers and seacoasts, the city-states of Italy and the communes of the North and West began to take form. They represented a powerful split in the social order, a violent deviation from feudalism.

Within the city the hereditary fuedal obligations began to lapse, and new organizations came about. The crafts and trades became organized as self-regulating guilds, corporate entities with great power, while the city itself became a quasi-independent political unit. The Hanseatic towns, the cities of north Italy, and others here and there over Europe, fought and bribed their way free of feudal obeisance. Their strength was due in part to the revival of trade, and it helped lay the basis for the emergence of the new nation-states. The city became a laboratory sheltered by walls of economic, military, and as a result, political, power, within which new forms of social order were developed. Constricting as that order may appear to us now, it was freedom and dignity to the serf. The Germans coined a phrase, "Stadtluft makt frei" (City air makes one free), which was literally true in many parts of Europe. After a year and a day in the city, the serf was freed of his hereditary estate: he was a free citizen of the urban community.

As a corporate entity the medieval European city responded to the needs of its people. In it developed new courts oriented to craft and commerce, which bypassed the rigid feudal courts of Church and Baron. In it developed also a system of taxation, a mode of self-government, a military system, and means of carrying out the age-old community housekeeping tasks. This system, compared with most of the cities of history, and certainly compared with the surrounding feudal countryside, was democratic and egalitarian. Membership in the city carried privileges and duties; it required the participation of everybody (if only in time of emergency), and it made possible the representation of most people in the government. From the corporate structure of the medieval commune many of our present notions of political life have developed.

The medieval cities became true centers of societies, however, only with great shifts in political power. To put it briefly, the rising monarchs who created nation-states used the concentration of wealth in the cities, even as they protected the cities against the surrounding and often hostile society of feudal agrarianism. As strongholds with organized manpower, wealth, and technologies, the cities were very important allies of the monarchs. In a world as poor, decentralized, and weak as western Europe in the fourteenth century, a city-state like Venice was a paramount power.

The continued consolidation of power in the new nation-states, however, slowly destroyed the autonomy of the cities. The invention of gunpowder, the growth of national sea-power and standing armies, eroded forever the great fortifications which had protected them. Fortunately for urban ways, this coincided with the erosion of the walls around the feudal castles. The nation-state welded into one large domain city and countryside, urbanite and peasant, lord and commoner. The new nation-states were not, however, particularly urban. Indeed, we may doubt if they were as urban as Rome under the Caesars. One authority notes that England as late as 1801 had less than 10 per cent of her population in cities of a hundred thousand or more, and England was far more urbanized than other European countries. (None achieved a comparable urban population before 1850.) [2] Our own society was overwhelmingly rural at the time of the American Revolution. Less than 5 per cent lived in cities, and only two cities (New York and Philadelphia) had as many as thirty thousand inhabitants.

In short, for most of history the city has been an island in a sea of rural life. Today, however, the United States

[2] See Kingsley Davis, "The Origin and Growth of Urbanization in the World," *American Journal of Sociology*, Vol. LX, No. 5, pp. 433 ff.

is 70 per cent urban, and our national life centers in the nineteen urban places with a population of a million or more. Contemporary societies are urban in a sense new to human history. How did this situation come about? What sustains it? What are some of the consequences? To answer these questions we will have to go beyond the dynamics that created the classic cities discussed: we will have to include forces that are transforming the very nature of human society and the human community.

Increase in Scale and Societal Transformation

Most of us today fail to grasp the significance of what has happened. We have an image of America which over-emphasizes the importance of the small town and the open country neighborhood. Our folk heroes are the Tom Sawyers and Huckleberry Finns of a lost America; our literature is replete with Thoreaus, Emersons, and Faulkners, who write of another world. Political folklore emphasizes the friends and neighbors, the rural virtues. Indeed, we are treated to the spectacle of city folk spending billions of dollars to maintain the family farm which they are persuaded is the backbone of the country, while most state legislatures are greatly biased toward the rural voters, thereby disfranchising many urbanites.

The reason for these rural survivals is simple: we have not been an urban nation for very long. As late as the 1890's most people lived outside the cities, while a very large proportion of urban dwellers today were born and raised in open country neighborhoods or in small towns permeated by the atmosphere of the countryside. Yet today a picture of America which concentrated on the 212 metropolitan areas and completely omitted the intervening landscape would be a fair enough map of the society. A majority of the people, the wealth, the labor force, and the power of the United States in the 1960's is concentrated in 1 per cent of the land area. Those who note our rapidly increasing population and speak of "standing room only" are the victims of a biased perspective. Spending their days in the city or its suburbs, driving its crowded throughways, they forget the continental spaces where men are rarer than wolves.

They also forget the dying small towns and depopulated rural neighborhoods. While the total population increases rapidly and the cities spread like tidal waves over their surrounding hinterlands, the small towns in between shrink and die or else become miniature metropolitan areas. The isolated farmhouses are vacated and ploughed under, as the total labor force employed in agriculture declines with every decennial census. (Today it is not much larger than the number of unemployed.) There is a great deal of space in America, but it lies in the enormous interstices between metropolitan regions. Within these regions we may feel crowded, for we are becoming a highly concentrated people.

ENERGY, TRANSPORTATION, AND THE CITY

Rapid metropolitanization is due to an overall change in the organization of our lives and work. Two major factors have made this possible. Both are changes in man's relationship with his enviroment, and together they have altered man's relationships with his fellow men. The two factors are (1) the discovery of new sources of energy, and (2) the changing space-time ratio. Each deserves a brief analysis.

Through most of human history the race has depended upon one form of energy only: the direct energy of the sun, stored in plants and transformed by the muscles of men and beasts. Upon this foundation were raised not only the society of the American Indians but that of Imperial Rome and Elizabethan England. And the limits of these societies are clear when we understand how little *surplus* energy, over and above the cost of gaining it, is available from this source. Today we have access to energy through new sources: the fossil fuels of the earth (coal and oil), the electricity available from falling water, the energy stored in radioactive matter. In short, the invention of the steam engine, which first released the energy in coal, was an event as momentous as the beginning of agriculture: it produced a great stream of surplus energy for human use.

In the process of using it we have revolutionized the earlier energy source, agriculture. We have increased productivity per man so rapidly that today one farmer does the work that two dozen did a few decades ago. At the same time the farmer who does this is dependent upon the products of the city: machines, fuel, fertilizer. These tools both make his tremendous productivity possible and bind him to the city in a way the peasant was never bound. Meanwhile the mass of the labor force, no longer tied to the cycle of plant and rain and sunlight, is free to use the newer energy sources in a vast and complex round of fabrication. In the factories of the city they fabricate jet airplanes, water skis, sun tan lotion, electric shoe-polishers, and other exotic bargains, as well as the age-old staples, food, clothing, and shelter.

At the same time, and closely related to the discovery of new energy sources, came increasing control of space. Men are today freer of spatial restraints than ever in the past. The real meaning of space is in the cost of traversing it, and space, which we think of as a barrier, may also be viewed as a channel for integrating the actions of men. The relation between space and cost we may dub the "space-time ratio," and it has been shrinking for the past several centuries. There is a hamlet about a half-hour's drive from Chicago called Half-day. It marked the place where our grandfathers, with buggy and team, stopped for lunch and a rest as they drove northwards towards Milwaukee. Today the citizen of Los Angeles can fly to San Francisco as quickly as he can drive from the airport to downtown Los Angeles. Modern societies are rapidly shrinking as the cost in time for traversing a given unit of miles moves downward from weeks to days to hours, and the communication of messages becomes almost instantaneous.

The consequences have been far-reaching. Let us emphasize one: the wider geographical areas over which human behavior can be organized. Organization, the allocation of tasks to different units and their integration in a coordinated system, depends heavily upon the ability to communicate and control. Today a network of human actors may spread over a continent and, through rapid transport and telecommunication, coordinate their actions as closely as if they were all in one city. Such possibilities of coordination were never present in the classic societies. The Roman governor was proconsular indeed: since he could not hear from Rome for a month or more, his actions were in effect the actions of the Consuls. Today the American ambassador in Moscow is not left long in doubt about the President's wish.

Taken together these two basic changes have allowed a radical shift in human organization. The network of interdependence which constitutes a human society can spread wider and maintain a more continuous flow of communication and a more dependable ordering of behavior than has ever been possible before. This widening of the network of interdependence is called *increase in societal scale*. It is the process which has radically transformed the small town America of Mark Twain into the metropolitan giant of today.

SOME CONSEQUENCES OF INCREASE IN SCALE

The increase in societal scale has meant rapid extension of the organizations that do the world's work. Business firms, oriented towards control of their resources, their markets, and their internal affairs have expanded rapidly.

This process, called integration, results in giant chains of corporations that control the automobile industry from the mining of coal and iron to the sale of the second-hand cars. Labor unions have developed in a parallel fashion: there is little point in dealing with a branch plant manager when the center of power is at the corporate headquarters, in New York or Detroit. As this occurs, relations between corporate and union giants lead to demands for governmental regulation: Big Government joins Big Business and Big Labor.

The process of organizational merger is too general to be confined to these examples. Organizational merger is the dynamic form of increase in scale. Through the growth of one network, or through the merging of several, giant systems develop which control the behavior of millions of men over thousands of miles and for decades of time. The competitive advantage of the larger enterprise, its greater ability to control the conditions necessary for survival, tends to abolish smaller competitors. Just as the small farmer gives up before huge industrial farms, so the household craft and industry give way to the factory. The "mommer n'popper" grocery store survives only through the long hours and low wages assigned to mama and poppa by themselves. The locally owned newspaper is bought on its deathbed by its competitor—part of a national enterprise.

At the headquarters and workshops of large-scale organization there is demand for the labor of those who leave the small enterprises. Freed from commitment to a family shop or farm, workers are drawn hither and thither across the continental society, moving towards labor shortages and economic booms. As this occurs a city is composed of a rich mixture of people from various parts of the country or even the world. Meanwhile, in the small town, the change in the space-time ratio has shortened the distance from farmer to city and the villages decline. The farmer flies from his Kansas wheat farm into Wichita in a private plane for shopping, medical care, or just golf and dinner and a

movie. On the other hand, cities with nationwide clienteles
arise: Miami Beach, Las Vegas, and other entertainment
centers, medical centers, university towns.

In short, increasing scale means an effective increase in
the size of our social world. Our lives become interdependent with those of millions of others; our horizons move
outward as we listen to messages from over the continent
or the world; our behavior is controlled by distant actors.
At the same time we have a greater freedom from our friends
and neighbors. If our basic necessities of life are provided
by membership in a giant corporation and union and
government, we have the freedom to withdraw from the
association. If pressed further we can move to a new neighborhood, or even a new city (in 1950, 24 per cent of the
people in Los Angeles were living at a different address
from the one they gave in 1949.) [3]

Thus urbanization, which in the past was largely the
same thing as the growth of cities, today means several
things. First, it means increase in scale, producing giant
organizations which attract large populations around their
headquarters and their workplaces. Second, it means the
growth of a new kind of culture, a way of life which is
based upon the national system and refers to that system.
This is urbanism in its broadest sense, the culture of urban
man. Finally, it means continued concentration in urban
areas. Increase in scale produces, in the words of Shevky
and Bell, both "an increase in the number and size of
cities," and "an increase in the range of functions centered
in cities."[4] Increase in scale makes cities possible and demands them as convenient sites to carry on the organized

[3] "Residential Mobility, 1949–1950, in the Ten Largest Standard Metropolitan Areas in the United States," Detroit Area Study, Survey
Research Center, University of Michigan, Project 843, No. 1211, May,
1957.
[4] Eshref Shevky and Wendell Bell, *Social Area Analysis,* Stanford:
Stanford University Press, 1955.

activities of the society: the allocation of tasks to different people and their integration in a coordinated system.

This great transformation has taken place in a very short time. Less than two hundred years ago the Constitution of the United States was framed by men whose economic and technological world was hardly different from that of Pericles. They rode horseback, derived power from plants and animal muscles, lived on farms scattered over the countryside, and (unlike the Athenian) often considered cities evil places. Today we try to apply their ideals of government to a nation in which the horse is a rarity known chiefly through western movies, power flows from coal, oil, electricity and the atom, and the farmer is a tiny minority of the population.

The Changing American Urban Community

Our cities today are the results and the expressions of broad changes in the total society. The growth of America might be described in these terms. First, the predominantly rural and scattered settlements of the colonies grew into dispersed and small-scale cities. Then an increasing flood of immigration settled the inland valleys with a sparse population. This immigration was followed by an increasingly rapid development of markets and workshops in the urban centers, leading to explosive growth with the harnessing of coal and steam. The growing network of railroads over the nation forged a continental society, with the workshops in the cities while the farms, forests, and mines became chiefly sources of raw materials. In this last phase the scattered population concentrated more and more in the great regional cities: Minneapolis-St. Paul, Chicago, St. Louis, Houston. Scattered regional populations regrouped in local metropolitan areas.

We tend to think of American growth as the product of

frontier development. However, the pioneer glamour of widespread farmers and ranchers who settled the interior valleys and the west should not blind us to some other considerations. The urban population of the United States has, since the early nineteenth century, consistently increased faster than the total population. While our population grew through immigration to virgin lands, the proportion of our people living in cities increased with each decade. For the United States entered history at a point when the scale of western society was already increasing rapidly. The colonies were settled as part of a worldwide empire, made possible by the increasingly effective use of sail to move merchandise over the seas. Our agriculture has always been oriented to a worldwide market. We have never had a peasantry of any importance, a subsistence economy of villages which could carry on independently of the cities. Nor have we ever had a feudal society whose remnants still survive in the contemporary politics and economies of some nations.

INCREASE IN SCALE AND THE DEVELOPMENT OF THE UNITED STATES

America was a new-found land at a new phase in the development of western civilization. Because it lacked the heritages of the past, it could take advantage of the many new sources of power and organization which emerged. Many traditions governing the use of people and land did not exist; others had shallow roots. The transplantation across the Atlantic weakened many traditional forms of order, the later melding of populations from every society in Europe further destroyed the hold of the older systems. In the United States Americans were, so to speak, de-civilized: their freedom from older restraint made possible a new ordering of the human units in a new system. With few taboos on the use of men, materials, and land Americans took full advantage of new relations between humanity and its environment brought about by the new technology. In the process they created a new set of relations among men.

American cities are a prime example of this freedom. They took shape on barren littorals, or at the place where paths crossed the broad inland rivers—Chicago spread over empty prairie like grass fire. They were built on land which had no history and no hallowed memories; instead of recalling the cathedrals of the bishops, the strongholds of royal families, the Roman camps, their names bring to mind only the campsites of wandering nomads, the meeting places of traders and tribesmen, the mythology of a dead and buried preliterate culture.

Americans, then, typically regard land not as place but as property. It is a site for human activities, a resource in economic enterprise. Thus the shape of American cities has varied greatly, shifting radically with each new development in the changing technology of transportation and building. We may, in fact, summarize the history of American cities in respect to their building layout by noting three great transportation revolutions. Each of these, in changing the mechanism for integrating various human activities over space, radically altered the relationships between the different localities within the city.

THE HISTORY OF OUR CITIES IN THE LIGHT OF TECHNOLOGICAL CHANGE

Most contemporary American cities grew to great size in the Age of Steam. The railroads, pushing into all the hinterlands of America, brought raw materials to the cities for processing and marketing. They also made possible the return to the farmer of ploughs, the McCormick reaper, barbed wire, guns, windmills—items which made easier the conquest of the prairies, and which the farmer could not provide for himself. But steam as a medium of transport has distinct limitations: the heavy engine requires rails, and these limit the places the train can go, while the motive force makes it impractical to stop and start very often. Thus the steam engine is well suited to hauling heavy goods for hundreds of miles, but it is poorly suited to short-haul transportation. As a consequence the city of the Age of Steam grew rapidly in size, for the space-time ratio among cities and between them and the hinterlands had decreased radically. But within the city the movement of men and goods went on in the ancient ways. Men walked, pulled, and hauled goods about, or used the horse-drawn vehicle. Because of the difficulty of movement, and the great and increasing amount of material to be moved, space in the city was at a premium.

Near the place where the railroads met the river or the sea, the heavy industry and warehouses clustered. Movement of the heaviest loads was reduced to a minimum. Near the workplace grew the row houses and tenement buildings that housed the workers, so that they could reach their jobs by walking. The shops and services that relied upon these populations and activities for trade, as well as those serving the entire city, were near the center. Other shops supplying necessities to the households were scattered through the city within walking distance of the various neighborhoods. Farther away from the noise and the unsightly workplaces came the neighborhoods of average housing, tall structures built close together with little yard space. Only the rich could afford so expensive a commodity as free space. With the ability to pay for space or transport, they built tall town houses in the center, or magniloquent testimonials to their wealth in the outlying districts. For the rich there was another possibility: railroad trains could and did stop every five or ten miles on their way out of the city. At these stops grew up the commuter towns, homes for the prosperous who had time to spend in commuting and money to pay the fare. The North Shore in

Chicago, the Main Line in Philadelphia, Westchester County in the New York area, are all monuments to the limits and uses of the railroad train for short-haul transport.

Lewis Mumford has called the city built during the Age of Steam the "paleotechnic city"—the city of older technologies.[5] He speaks of its basic components as the factory and the slums, and indeed the housing for workers was dark and congested while their hours, pay, and working conditions would appall contemporary Americans. They were, like space, exploited by the new organizational commanders, who developed power and wealth upon the base of the great technological break-throughs.

The City of Steam was developed during the nineteenth century. From its beginnings, however, entrepreneurs had seen the widespread need and the potential market for short-haul transport. This developed also upon rails. First the horse-cars drawn along rails set in streets, then the cable cars attached to a continuous moving cable, finally the electric railway with power supplied by a third rail or an overhead electric conductor, made it easier to get about within the burgeoning structure of the city. By the second decade of this century the great cities had complex spiderwebs of electric railways crossing at the center, the downtown area. These lines brought about a tremendous movement of trade towards the center. At the same time they allowed the development of vast new neighborhoods along the spokes of the transportation grid. Between the spokes, however, still lay large undeveloped areas, uneconomical for the electric railway and therefore for residential building. Movement was still tied to the rigid line of the rails, the "right of way."

The City of the Streetcar was hardly complete before the instrument of its destruction appeared. The automobile was an oddity in the years before World War I; by the end

[5] In *Technics and Civilization*, New York: Harcourt, Brace, and Company, 1934.

of the 1920's it was a commonplace mode of travel for those
of middle income or more; by the 1930's it was becoming
nearly universal; today it is almost a necessity. Freed of the
rails and of the requirement of collective movement, each
person derived a tremendous liberty from the automobile.
He could move at will, at any time, wherever the public
streets led. And the greater the number of auto owners,
the greater the demand for streets. As the streets were developed, the housing followed (though sometimes the se-
quence was reversed), and the interstices between the
spokes of the streetcar lines were rapidly filled. Settlement
moved far out beyond the boundaries of the old city, following highways into the country towns, and when this
occured the country towns became *de facto* parts of the
greater metropolis.

With the widespread adoption of the automobile, we
come to the third city: the centrifugal metropolis. The
increasing dependence on the automobile at first improved
the commercial position of downtown business, but it soon
became apparent that the ancient streets, developed for
foot and streetcar traffic, could hardly handle the floods
of cars, while space for parking became a serious problem
to the casual shopper. At the same time the automobile-
based settlements at the outer edge went further and further
from the center, increasing the driving time. As this occured, two series of efforts were launched. One was intended
to make the downtown more accessible by building giant
throughways from the peripheries to the center, with great
interchanges at the center allowing people to move out
to any part of the city. The other was the development of
circumferential highways around the outskirts of the city,
allowing much traffic to bypass the downtown altogether.

THE DISPERSION OF THE CITY

The new neighborhoods on the peripheries once more
presented a profitable market for the local enterprise. On

the outskirts of the cities, in the new tract developments, planned shopping centers began to appear after World War II. Their clustered goods and services made available to the suburbanite the same convenience neighborhood centers had monopolized before the Age of the Streetcar. Convenience shopping moved, voluminously, from downtown out to the suburbs. Where the major arterials to the downtown crossed the cuicumferentials, however, the shopping centers which were developed approximated in range of goods and services those of the downtown center itself. The centrifugal metropolis spawned dozens of subcities on its edges, while the downtown gradually ceased to be the center of wealth and the show window of the complex.

This brings us to the city as we know it today, a changing structure which still bears in outline the remnants of the Age of Steam and the star-shaped City of the Streetcar. Much of our present city is, in fact, caught in a conflict between the cities of the past and the city of the future. Though we do not have the historical commitments of European nations to older social and political structures, we have our own urban history: it is a history of rapidly changing technology which destroys as it creates. The sentiments and symbols of American urbanites are forever being destroyed to make way for the new.

Suggested Readings

On the City in Time and Space:

The Great Cultural Traditions, Ralph Turner, New York: McGraw-Hill Book Company, 1941. A brilliant comparative survey of the early city-states and the classical empires, with analysis of the causes and results of urbanization in the age of agricultural dominance.

Medieval Cities: Their Origins and the Revival of Trade, Henri Pirenne, Garden City, N.Y.: Doubleday and Company, Anchor Edition. A classic in the study of the revival of urban centers in the feudal society which followed the decay of the Roman system. The "island city" is portrayed as part of the societal order, yet apart from it in certain crucial respects.

On Increase in Scale and Societal Transformation

Energy and Society, Fred Cottrell, New York, McGraw-Hill Book Company, 1955. A thorough analysis of the effects of technological change upon social structure, with primary concern for transport, communication, and energy transformation. (This is also available in a paperback edition.)

The Emerging City: Myth and Reality, Scott Greer, New York: The Free Press of Glencoe, Inc., 1962. A sociological study of the modern city, a larger work expanding much of the author's present discussion.

On the Changing American Urban Community

The Exploding Metropolis, by the editors of *Fortune,* Garden City, N.Y.: Doubleday and Company, Anchor Edition, 1958. A topical and provocative discussion of the problems of the big city, from a point of view friendly to the great cities of the nineteenth century.

Social Organization, Scott Greer, New York: Random House, 1955. A brief analytical theory of social organization. In the final chapter, "The Changing Organizational Topography," recent history is seen within the framework emphasizing the continual trend towards the increase in scale of large, formal organizations. In sum, these lead to the dominance of the national system over the local community and the specialized group.

2

The People of
the Metropolis

The dynamic forces producing the metropolis have created great differences among urban people. Increase in
scale, the process which built the organizational network
in which the city is the "knot", has three major aspects,
each of which results in greater social differences among
the citizens. As scale increases, populations hitherto separated are united in one network of order; there is a vast
proliferation in the number and kinds of tasks within
the larger system; there is a consistent tendency for the
work of the world to be performed by larger organizations,
culminating in the world-spanning corporate giants. Each
of these changes profoundly affects the everyday life and
times of the citizen.

VARIATION OF URBAN LIVES: ETHNICITY, SOCIAL RANK,
AND LIFE STYLE

As the society expands, scattered and diverse groups are
brought within one network of control. This comes about

23

through the melding of nearby populations in the growing order (as occured with the country towns on the outskirts of a city, or with the Sabines who lived near the city of Rome). It also comes about through migration, the movement of people from outside areas into the system. Both processes have been important in America. Close integration of the regions has brought the problems of race relations in Alabama into the northern home and classroom, while union-management relations in Chicago have become a topic in the South. Furthermore, closer integration of the national system has greatly encouraged the migration of people from one region to another. Thus Southerners, Negro and white, have moved in a steady stream from the Southeast towards St. Louis, Baltimore, Los Angeles. In New York's Harlem and Chicago's South Side, Negroes originally from the South have built massive cities within cities.

Equally important has been the growth of the national system and its cities through immigration. During the floodtide, as many as one million immigrants a year entered the United States. They came in stages. In the early days came the people from Great Britian, Ireland, Germany—in short, northern and western Europe. Then came those from Italy, Poland, Russia—southern and eastern Europe, Finally, in the past three decades, we have experienced a massive immigration of persons from Mexico and Puerto Rico.

Thus the city of a large-scale society is a polyglot mosaic of national and regional cultures. Every nationality of any size on earth is represented in New York City. Every language is spoken. These strangers, coming from the various tundras, savannahs, steppes, and heaths of the earth, bring with them distinct and unique histories, sacred symbols, ways of life. Their gods are different from those of the host society and from those of other newcomers. Furthermore, many of them come from a biological stock that varies from those who have already arrived and from fellow immigrants. Though mankind varies less biologically than does one subspecies of Spider Monkey, human beings in their narcissism are extremely self-conscious about minor variations in looks. So the growing population of the large-scale metropolis may seem as heterogeneous as the birds and beasts of the jungle. *This kind of social differentiation is known as ethnicity.*

The tremendous increase in the division of labor with expanding scale creates a society where citizenship is based upon "the job." In simple societies like that of the peasant village, a dozen occupations exhausted the opportunities a self-respecting man had to make a living. Even the America of Jefferson's day was not much more varied. In our society, estimates place the number of kinds of jobs at thirty-five thousand and up, each of them a distinct part of the necessary work in some social enterprise. Similarity of occupation and near-equality among a few broad classes of workers have given way to wide distances between many occupational worlds. The research physicist who lives near the advertising executive, the small business man, and the city councilman, can share with them an evening in the swimming pool; he cannot share his professional problems, or his professional code and folkways. Nor do they all share equal rewards. They are separated in these respects by social distance.

Upon the basis of the job a person receives his share of the social surplus, the economic goods and services available. In qualifying for his job, he reaches some level of skill and general expertise; he must be educated to some level. Furthermore, once he is within the world of the job he shares a way of looking at things, of conceptualizing and evaluating, which is unique to this kind of job and to no other. In other words physicists, advertising executives, small business men, politicians, develop little cultural worlds of their own, or subcultures. When, therefore, we say that the change in the nature of work affects the differences among men, we refer to three interconnected variations which all relate to the job. Putting them in the simplest everyday language, they are variations in occupation, education, and income. As a general kind of social differentiation, this is known as *social rank*.

The increasing importance of large-scale organizations in doing the world's work results in another kind of variation. With the rise of vast bureaucracies in the extraction, fabrication, and marketing of material goods, as well as in government and other areas of our common life, there has been a decline of the small enterprise. The latter was, in the past, often a family enterprise. Family farm and shop and store are disappearing today, leaving a labor force to be reorganized as factories in the fields (the term for the giant land companies of California), assembly-line manufacturing, or chain supermarkets. With the disappearance of family enterprise, however, we are separating completely two great organizational realms of human society: kinship and work.

The separation of the worlds of kinship and work has several major effects upon our lives. First, it means that we are free to live completely outside the boundaries of a kinship. In many small-scale societies membership in a large network of kinship was a person's only claim on the land and therefore on a living; to be outside the family was to die. In large-scale society we can disregard the relatives entirely, for we sell only our own actions to a large organization which cares not at all for our relatives. Second, this separation means that we need not even enter into conjugal family relations; even if we marry, we need not have children for there is no formal or informal constraint that forces it. Thus Americans range from those with large families to those without children and even without a marriage partner. A third major result is the separation of work place and residence; the sites for economic activity and family activity may lie on opposite sides of the metropolis. This means that the effects of one upon the other tend to be minimized, for the two kinds of relationships are insulated. A person works as an isolated, non-family individual.

The separation of work from kinship allows a wide latitude for individual choice. People at the same level of social rank, with similar jobs and resources, may choose to live in single bliss (or married without children, or with a single child), spending their leisure and economic surplus on the various avocations and amusements available in the city. They will have little need for large space, and they are likely to live near the center in the apartment house complexes. Theirs is an urbane mode of life. On the other hand, they may marry, cherish children, and therefore require private space, indoors and out. In this case they are likely to be found in single-family houses, and to care a great deal about owning their homes. Theirs is a familistic way of life. This kind of variation among a population has been called *life-style,* or variation along the *familism-urbanism* continuum.

We have discussed these three kinds of variations at some length because they are basic in understanding the urban residents who must be governed. We have taken each dimension separately, and indeed they are not necessarily connected. *Ethnicity, social rank,* and *life style* may each vary independently of the remaining dimensions, just as length can vary independently of height, and thickness independently of either, in a sculpture, a building, or a cloud. Historically, however, they have been connected. In the period of most rapid proportional increase in the scale of American society, around 1900, all three dimensions tended to go together. This was because a great many people were coming into the urban centers from the small towns of the hinterlands and the small towns and villages of European nations. They came in without much experience of urban life, without much education (many foreign-born immigrants could not even speak English), and with ways of acting and life-styles developed in familistic rural society. Thus ethnicity, social rank, and life-style all went together among the newest migrants.

We might speak of two polar examples to clarify the point. At one extreme were the newer migrants, the first generation from southern and eastern Europe. They spoke strange languages and broken English, their religions (chiefly Judaism, Orthodox Christianity, or Catholicism), were different from English faiths, their national traditions were alien. With little formal education and few skills, they had to take the lowest-level jobs, which demanded little and paid little. And, tending to perpetuate their small town way of life. they centered much of their surplus time, energy, and money upon their family. In some cases this even included the extended family, uncles and aunts and "cousins by the dozens," for entire villages and clans moved intact from the old country to certain American cities. At the other extreme we might imagine the "Old American" family, originally from Great Britain, Protestant in religion, Anglo-Saxon in cultural background. Such families had been here longer; they tended to have better educations for the urban milieu, and consequently occupied the higher level jobs and received the better rewards. In becoming acculturated to the city they left behind much of the countryman's concern with kin and kinder; their way of life was more urbane.

INCREASING SOCIAL CHOICE AND VARIATIONS IN URBAN LIVES

Such a picture is greatly oversimplified. However, it makes the important point that the three dimensions of variation were highly intercorrelated. They tended to go together. The more urban the population, the higher its social rank, the fewer its children; and the reverse was also true. In such a society the various subareas of the city were indeed, as Park calls them, "a mosaic of words which touch but do not interpenetrate." Moving from Little Sicily to the Polish Corridor, from Germantown to the Ghetto, from the Main Line or North Shore to the Bowery, was to move from one incapsullated and bounded subworld to another. Today, however, the three dimensions of urban differentiation are no longer so closely related. The *analytical separateness,* the logical distinctness between them which we noted earlier, has become a real separation: ethnicity, social rank, and life-style all vary in contemporary American cities, and each varies independently of the others.

The reasons are again implicit in the great processes of change involved when scale increases. The continued delegation of work to large-scale bureaucracies, utilizing new energy sources and machines, requires a continual improvement in the average job of the labor force. It becomes more demanding of thought and skill. The result is a decline in the demand for unskilled labor. At the same time free public education has greatly improved the average man's chance for a high school education. The economy has increased its productivity, and there are more rewards for all. Education, occupation, and income have all increased. The vast ethnic segments of the population have benefited from these trends. At the same time, the closing of immigration in the 1920's to most nationalities means that today those bearing the signs of foreign birth are about to disappear. Their children are not easily distinguishable from the other people of the city. In time newcomers to the city, from American small towns or from Italy and Poland, abandon their efforts to continue an older, familistic way of life. Automatic conformity to the old life-style gives way to a free choice along the continuum from urbanism to familism as ways of life.

Thus the contemporary population of the metropolis is less like a patchwork quilt, with sharp boundaries separating those who differ sinultaneously on all three counts, and more like a single woven fabric. Though an individual's nationality of origin still makes a difference in the friends he has and the things he does, the differences are muted and softer. The grandchild of the Sicilian does not stand out, as his grandfather did, among his own age groups.

With higher education and income levels, even the blue-collar worker differs less from the professional or manager than was the case a short while ago. Increasing social surplus, resulting from increase in scale, allows (1) more material goods and services, (2) more leisure time, and (3) more access to the flow of communication in the society through literacy and the mass media, for all of the occupational levels of the metropolis. In the process the more dramatic differences disappear. Thirty-five years ago the Lynd's describing a midwestern city, spoke of a six-day, sixty-hour work week for factory hands, without a vacation. Today the work week averages less than forty hours, and the annual vacation of two or three weeks is nearly universal. Heavy, unskilled labor is rapidly disappearing with the increase in mechanization. Off the job, it is frequently difficult to distinguish between executive, accountant, and machine operator. And during the summer, in the National Park, they park their trailers side by side and seem to enjoy similar experiences.

Such a blurring of class and nationality differences does not mean they have disappeared. Nobody who drives the length of a metropolitan area can fail to be impressed by the great differences in size and quality of housing, as well as style of dwelling unit. There remain substantial average differences in income for different occupational levels (or *strata* as they are called by analogy with geological layers), and these differences are translated into a major reward in our society, the family dwelling place. The family home, however, rarely stands out from its background: rich man, poor man, beggar man, and thief rarely live side by side. Houses are like their neighborhoods, and neighborhoods are, in turn, like the larger local communities within the metropolis. How does this come about?

The Map of the Metropolis and the Division of Rewards

The map of the contemporary urban area is a dramatic example of a geographical division of labor. A complex and enormous network of activity is separated into component parts and carried on at different spatial locations. The results are all coordinated. At the same time the major part of the space is allocated to the endless seas of houses, the residential areas of the city. It is probably true that no fact about a person will tell you as much about his general place in the world and his behavior as the single fact of his job. When Americans meet strangers, their first question is typically "What do you do?" After the job, however, the residential address is a strong candidate for second place. Where you live tells those persons with information about a city such things as your general income level, the kind of people you live among, your probable prestige or social honor, and any number of less basic matters.

Of course it does not tell with precision much about your temperament or character. These are not social facts, whereas the permanent residential address is a social fact and highly correlated with other important social facts such as those noted above. It is produced by the housing market, the mechanism which allocates rewards in the shape of homes, in the metropolis. The importance of those rewards is evident in the sometimes violent struggles for different and better housing carried on by the Negroes and other ethnic groups. Their importance is also manifest in the fierce resistance to "invasion" of a neighborhood by a different kind of people. The family home is, in most cases, all that the average American ever achieves of private property; his attachment to it may be the basis for the popular sacredness of that concept. The home is both his score in the game of success and his most precious asset.

Neighborhoods tend to be inhabited by families of roughly similar social rank because they have the same price for the same kind of housing. This comes about since the site as a scene for human action lies a specific distance from given structures—workplaces, markets, and the like, including nuisances like heavy industry—and has a specific kind of topography. These are translated by bids for the ownership and use of the land (in other words, the market) into a given price level per lot. The price level in turn sets the limits within which housing is built.

We have already discussed briefly the building layout in the City of Steam. It is a settlement where workplaces lie near the rivers and the railroads, and near them are the houses of the workers. Such residential areas are not very attractive to most Americans for they tend to be in the lowlands near water, while nearby are the noisy, dirty, and odoriferous plants of heavy industry. They are, however, admirably suited to reducing the amount of time the worker spends in going to and from his job. As a person moves away from these centers of activity the land's altitude and prestige increase, and with these increases go larger and more expensive houses with carriage circles and gardened estates.

The ruins of this city still exist in the centers of our older urban complexes, but the changes brought about by increase in scale have greatly modified the values on which it was based. The increasing economic surplus has allowed millions of families more resources and greater choice for housing: a person who buys a new structure has more control over his residence than one who rents. At the same time, as social choice with respect to life-style has increased, a larger and larger proportion of urban dwellers have chosen a familistic way of life. Committed to home and children, they need private space indoors and out, and the row houses and crowded three-flat structures of the central city are obsolete. At the same time, the change in the space-time ratio brought about by widespread distribution of automobiles has meant that enormous new spaces on the peripheries of the city can be developed as neighborhoods.

THE INHERITED CITY AND THE CHANGING NEIGHBORHOODS

Thus the contemporary metropolitan area differs greatly from center to periphery. The grid of housing opportunities shows decreasing density as we move outwards into the areas of new building. The suburban rings are typically dispersed, with neighborhoods composed entirely of detached single-family houses surrounded by yard and patio. Here live the grandchildren of the immigrants, the white-collar workers and factory workers, professionals and entrepreneurs, for the great expansion in available housing sites meant that familistic neighborhoods could be built for the different social ranks, from semiskilled workers on up. Here live all those who have chosen a familistic life-style, whatever their level of occupation, income, and education. The suburbs, once homes of the wealthy commuters, are today a broad slice of the middle and upper ranks of urban society. They have in common only a commitment to familism, to children, home, and neighborhood.

The older central city, however, is heavily committed to structures and uses inherited from the past. It remains the center of work. Most suburban residents still travel inwards to work, and this is particularly true of those with the highest social rank, the most skilled and honored jobs, the greatest rewards. The city is also still a center of the national organization and the metropolis-wide markets, though certain types of commercial activity are decentralizing rapidly, with the neighborhood shopping centers taking over the rich suburban market in family consumables.

The central city also retains a monopoly of the older,

denser, residential neighborhoods. Because of the attraction of newer alternatives, the bright ranch-style houses on the peripheries, a wide band of urban population which once lived near the center now lives in the suburbs. Vast segments of the central city are termed "grey areas," they are not slums, either physically or socially, and they are not apt to be razed by the demand for space to house new developments. They are simply declining in market value. In these areas, halfway between the center and the peripheries, are found a large proportion of the manual workers of the city's labor force. And here also are found those ethnic minorities who, like the Mexican-Americans, are new to the city and therefore poorly equipped to cope in terms of social rank. Finally, in the grey areas and the slums,—in the black belt of Chicago, the Hill of Pittsburgh, Harlem in New York—are found the huge and growing population of ethnics segregated on the basis of skin color. Negroes and Puerto Ricans, whatever their social rank and acculturation to the ways of the city, cannot choose the familistic suburban neighborhood, for they are disbarred, legally and illegally, from the move outward. Consequently land values in the city are still high for such segregated groups.

On the outer edges of the old central city are many neighborhoods indistinguishable from those of the suburbs. They were the last to be built within the city's boundaries, and they were usually of upper social rank from their beginnings. Thus they have the qualities of private space and distance from workplaces which give them a suburban air. Here are populations of middle to high social rank, low ethnicity, and familistic life-styles. In fact there is little difference between the outlying city neighborhoods and the suburbs nearest the urban border.

Indeed, we must not think of the central city and the suburbs as absolute contrasts. To be sure, the central area tends to have a monopoly of the very poor and the ethnic populations, just as the suburbs have most of the wealthy residents of a metropolis. But these two extremes account for only a fraction of the total population in a giant metropolitan complex; the other two-thirds are the middle-ranges of social rank, those who were once entirely within the central city's boundaries. The familistic neighborhoods are not all suburban, nor are most central city dwellers highly urban in their style of life. While the central city has a monopoly of the highly urban populations, the majority of its people are still family-centered, home-centered, child-rearing populations.

The suburbs are today predominantly at the familistic end of the life-style continuum. They are middle to upper social rank. They are the home of the great middle range of American society. Though many of their residents are from families that were originally ethnic, the process of acculturation has blurred these distinctions. Irish, Italian, Hungarian, and German—the names linger on, but they have a new meaning in the middle-rank, familistic neighborhoods of the suburban community. The central city may look radically different, but if we are careful to avoid literary stereotypes we will find that most central city people are just about the same as most suburbanites.

The Maintenance of Order in the Urban Community

Lately some have argued that the metropolitan complex is in no meaningful sense a unity. They point out its loss of autonomy: it has no military or foreign relations, it is a creature of the State with little governmental freedom. The growth of the larger system has merged it in a set of relationships making it utterly dependent upon the entire nation. That growth has also meant that most of the important affairs of its citizens, most social tasks, are carried out by giant, specialized, formal organizations. These do not involve many citizens of one city, but they span dozens of cities with organizational structures, and those committed to them as members and publics give only a subordinate loyalty to their local area. The organizations in turn have no reason to care about one specific city: they are natives of many, so transients in all.

As a consequence, so the argument runs, the urban area is simply a site. Upon this site, individuals with the most heterogeneous and disparate loyalties and concerns go their separate ways, with little concern for the common welfare or the fate of the city. For this reason there can be no community, no common order and common commitment to the area as a social whole. Interdependence is no longer a result of residence in any one place, nor is that structure of rights and duties called a normative order based upon living there. Consequently, the things that move and constrain men do not have their roots in any particular city; they result from the giant bureaucracies of large-scale society. Eighty per cent of our labor force works for such bureaucracies, and he who pays the piper calls the tune.

This argument is so plausible, and at so many points consistent with our argument from the nature of increasing scale, that one tends to ignore some of the assumptions involved. When the assumptions are questioned, however, a new definition of the city emerges. To see it, we must first consider what is meant by a social order, cease to take for granted all of the routine, predictable behavior of men, and all the efforts at accommodation and peaceful cooperation. Instead we ask: how does this order come about, and what keeps it alive?

THE CITY AS A PROBLEM OF SOCIAL ORDER

The city is a maze, a social zoo, a mass of heterogeneous social types. They come from the four corners of the earth. Much of their behavior is completely beyond the understanding of any one actor, and they are related in a thousand different ways. Their city teems with conflict and hums with tension: Negroes fight for housing and jobs, landlords fight the housing inspectors and their tenants, gangs of adolescents terrify entire neighborhoods, men of violence terrify entire labor unions and industries.

To make the latent conflict sharp and clear, we have only to travel the few miles from the Negro ghetto (Harlem, the Chicago South Side) to the enclaves of the upper classes (Westchester County in New York, the North Shore suburbs in Chicago), keeping our eyes open to differences in social rank, honor, wealth, the accoutrements of life. It is a journey that thousands of Negro servants make every day. Or, from another perspective, look at the hundred thousand automobiles travelling an arterial throughway during the rush hour, or read statistics on the mountains of food and materials which must be moved into New York City every twenty-four hours. Here is a massive order maintained among enormous variation. To account for this order, we shall have to consider the urban complex as far more than a convenient resting together of many people in a small space.

SOLUTIONS TO THE PROBLEM OF ORDER

Our impatience with the existing order, our hopes for a better one, may blind us to the magnitude of our achievements. Let us look at the metropolis and ask one question: how is this vast array of behavior among a heterogeneous mass organized and made predictable, so that trains pull into the city before dawn and the people are fed? First, and most easily, we can say that within the boundaries of clearly defined membership groups order is relatively explicable. Out of interdependence grows communication through a role system and norms. Jobs, morals, and rules of the road tell people what to do. This communication leads to an ordering of behavior, one that perpetuates the organization. Such an approach explains much about the internal order of a group—public school, corporation, household, or labor union. We have a growing theoretical understanding of the single organization looked at as a system.

Such understanding, however, is not enough. Order within groups tells us little about order between them. It is even possible that the greater the control within organizations the greater the chaos in their relationships with each other. (Look, for example, at the relationships between nation-states.) And intergroup order is crucial in the urban area for two reasons. First, some groups cannot perform their tasks at all without predictable cooperation from others—workers and managements, schools and families, businesses and customers. Second, external groups may easily block the activity crucial to the continuation of any one group's enterprise: the tannery and slaughterhouse can move into an area and destroy its value for the real estate firm, or the organized gang of teen-age hoodlums can make a playground unusable.

Order outside the bounds of the bureaucracies is required at another point. Cities are filled with spaces between groups. In places of public aggregation, in parks and playgrounds, on the city sidewalks and streets, we are not members of any known group. There is no prescribed communication system, and we have no way of sanctioning the actions of others. The city population is various, and many do not always agree with us about what is right and proper. Yet millions of us spend minutes or hours each day in such public places, outside the organizational walls of work or home where automatic order can be expected. In short, there is an inescapable area of social interaction with no social group to order it.

Two radically different types of organization are involved in that social order called the city. The first we have discussed: the large-scale, specialized, formal organizations which control segments of our behavior and do much of the world's work. They span cities, states, nations; they are completely responsible for none of these. They are exclusive, concerned with only some people in any city, and only some aspects of their behavior. Yet they must be established somewhere; they must have offices, plants, stores. And wherever they go they have neighbors, they have property to protect, and business contracts to enforce, and paths to walk down city streets at night. In short, they are dependent upon an order which they alone cannot maintain. That order is maintained by the second type of social organization.

THE BASIS OF URBAN ORDER: THE LOCAL POLITICAL COMMUNITY

The order of the local political community is the product of an *spatially inclusive* organization. Such an organization grows out of the interdependence among those persons committed to a given scene for human action. It establishes rights and duties in the areas crucial to the common life. It develops a basis for punishment in that same interdependence. And, on the basis of interdependence, such an organization develops formal agencies, mechanisms for maintaining the site. To the tasks of maintaining public order and the safety of persons by policing the organizational interstices and by arbitrating conflict between organized groups, are added the basic housekeeping duties of the city.

Some tasks growing out of the dense concentration of highly interdependent populations are inescapable. The transport system must have a certain speed, capacity, and predictability in circulating men, goods, and messages. (Without transport a city would be merely a scatteration of villages, unable to combine and therefore unable to achieve a division of labor.) The flow of water from its sources to the population must be guaranteed, as must the disposal of the collective waste, a massive problem in any city. A minimal level of public health and protection against fire are closely associated with these tasks: sanitation is related to the first, water supply to the second. To these are added, in various amounts, other public facilities— parks, museums, theatres, and monuments—but the basic necessities for continual operation of the enterprise are those listed above.

Thus two sorts of tasks are carried out through the inclusive territorial organization: the maintenance of order beyond and outside the exclusive membership organization, and the maintenance of the plant, the common site. Both are chiefly the responsibility of local government in our metropolitan areas today. Public order between interdependent groups is maintained by the development of a role system at a higher level. In this system, groups and social categories are the actors. Their rights and duties are spelled out and sanctions are applied through the police power ordered by the courts. The safety of person and property is maintained by that peculiarly urban role system, the police force. In the anonymity of mass interaction in public aggregates there is no social group whose members, through punishments and rewards, or threats and promises, control each other's behavior. Yet a rough system of rights and duties is defined in the law. The police officer is the general substitute for that group: *our* rights become *his* duties, and our duties, his rights.

We have noted that the maintenance of the scene is not as clearly defined in scope as the maintenance of order. This is because many of the tasks traditionally assigned to government could probably be carried out by some other kind of organization *if the market would permit*. Early highways in America were private enterprises in many cases, paid for by users through a toll. Parks and playgrounds, as we know, need not be public. In short, the government as entrepreneur and developer, as an economic force maintaining the plant of the metropolis, is much less inescapable than it is in its role as guarantor and enforcer of order.

We cannot escape the political nature of the order in its latter role. The localized world of the metropolis could conceivably be administered by a proconsul from Washington, D.C., or the state capitol. It could not be operated by a private enterprise. Its function is the adjustment of conflict among the corporate citizens and social categories of the area. This conflict is real, the stakes may be very high, and the final question is no less than this: Who is a first class citizen, and whose interests shall prevail in this area? Such questions are not answered by simple administrative routine; they cannot be answered in a laboratory or with an electronic computer. They can be answered only through a political process which is accepted as legitimate, and which can make binding decisions enforceable by the police power and the public treasury of the society.

Suggested Readings

On the Variation of Urban Lives and Social Choice

Social Area Analysis, Eshref Shevky and Wendell Bell, Stanford: Stanford University Press, 1955. A technical discussion of the emergence of three dimensions along which urban populations vary—ethnicity, social rank, and life style—with a demonstration of one method for identifying and measuring these dimensions. The theoretical essay in the beginning is difficult but repays close study because of the scope and penetration of analysis.

"Social Choice, Life Style, and Suburban Residence," Wendell Bell, in W. A. Dobriner, editor, *The Suburban Community*, New York: G. P. Putnam's Sons, 1958. A discussion of the consequences of increased choice of residence and way of life, based upon the study of two Chicago suburban areas. The reader in which this piece is included is also useful, since it includes a wide variety of essays on suburban social structure.

On the Map of the Metropolis and the Division of Rewards

Cities and Society, The Revised Reader in Urban Sociology, Paul K. Hatt and Albert J. Reiss, Jr., editors, Glencoe, Ill.: The Free Press of Glencoe, Inc., 1957. This is an authoritative collection of empirical studies of the city, with some attention to seminal essays which have affected that research in the past. Much of the reader is devoted to spatial distributions of activities and people.

Studies in Human Ecology, George A. Theodorson, editor, Evanston, Ill.: Row, Peterson and Company, 1961. A more recent collection, this reader carries a wide variety of articles detailing the relationships between social activity and spatial location; these include an important section of social area analysis.

On The Maintainance of Order in the Urban Community

The Death and Life of Great American Cities, Jane Jacobs, New York: Random House, 1961. In this ingenious and original essay, the social basis for order and growth at the level of the neighborhood and local community within the metropolis is analysed in a lively fashion. In the process the author attacks many current dogmas which are used by professional planners as well as laymen (and develops some of her own.)

The Community Press in an Urban Setting, Morris Janowitz, Glencoe, Ill.: The Free Press, Inc., 1952. Janowitz describes the social structure of several central city "local communities" within the Chicago metropolitan complex. He discusses their boundaries, their persistence, and their power to order the behavior of their residents. Though the community paper is important as a transmitter of communication, it depends for its value upon an existing social community.

Part II

The Governmental

Response to

Metropolitanization

3

The Governmental
Mosaic of the
Metropolis

Late in the last century a distinguished commentator on American life noted that municipal government was the one conspicuous failure of our society. Coming from Britain, where local government is administered by the middle class in terms of its understanding of the general welfare, Lord Bryce was shocked.[1] American cities, with elaborate machinery for enforcing democracy, were run by gangs. Tammany Hall shamelessly bribed, corrupted, and sold out the policy of New York City to the highest bidder. The men who ran our governments operated by a moral code whose chief distinction was that between "honest graft" and "dishonest graft." (The immortal phrase is from Plunkitt of Tammany Hall, whose self-designed epitaph

[1] James Bryce, *The American Commonwealth*, London and New York: Macmillan and Company, 1889.

45

was "He seen his opportunities and he took them.") [2] Enormous contracts were sold for private income; criminals bought hunting licenses from the police; ordinary enterprise paid tribute to the *condottieri* of City Hall.

There is more to this picture, however. Seth Low, Mayor of Brooklyn at the time of Lord Bryce's visit, appends a rebuttal to the last edition of the Englishman's book. Eloquently, he makes a major point. At whatever cost in plunder and crime, the cities of America in the last half of the nineteenth century grew tenfold. Urban population increased from less than four million to more than thirty million. A rapidly growing nation which was 15 per cent urban in 1850 was 40 per cent urban by the turn of the century. It was a true population explosion. And as Low points out, these floods of people were housed, order was maintained, streets were built, transport was established, water was brought in, and wastes were carried away. What wonder that many mistakes were made? More impressive is the over-all achievement. The fantastic expansion of the urban plant in nineteenth century America is one of the most striking examples of collective achievement.

Lord Bryce, however, might still retort, "Yes, but at what a cost." And most of the unnecessary cost of that development was due to governmental structure inadequate to the burdens of explosive urbanization. To understand this we must look at American definitions of municipal government. These were the rules, inherited from the past, codified in law and the state constitutions, which set the limits within which our urban governments could develop. They were quite inadequate to the floods of history.

THE NORMS OF LOCAL GOVERNMENT IN THE UNITED STATES

American cities ceased to be administered by appointed delegates of the state after the Revolutionary War. Instead,

[2] George Washingeon Plunkitt, *Plunkitt of Tammany Hall* (as recorded by William Riordan), New York: McClure-Philips and Company, 1905.

an effort was made to combine dominance by the state legislatures with Jacksonian democracy. At the price of considerable simplification, let us say that Jacksonian ideology was translated into these norms. (1) The city was responsible to the ordinary citizen through universal manhood suffrage; (2) office was open to all and could be managed successfully by any citizen; (3) the citizens had a sacred right to local self-rule. The results were chiefly visible in the incompetence and peculation common to urban government. With massive public works, a flood of culturally illiterate new citizens, and the exposure of all key offices to the electorate, government became a key form of private enterprise to its practitioners. And, because of their interdependence within the urban area, many nonpolitical persons were drawn willy-nilly into the "ring" that ran the city. The basic ambivalence between local self-rule and the doctrine that the legal city was merely a creature of the State led to frequent special and discriminatory acts at the state capitol. The big, wicked city was deemed incapable of governing itself. State legislatures responded with "ripper legislation" aimed at destroying powers of the city. Some major cities, such as Memphis and Mobile, were actually abolished. The police force of St. Louis is still partially controlled from Jefferson City, the little capitol city of Missouri.[3]

At the same time, the state constitutions provided easy means of incorporating new municipalities. Under the "right to local self-rule," state constitutions also specified extremely difficult processes for annexation or amalgamation of existing cities. Furthermore, translation of this right into political form meant that the city was required to gain the consent of the citizens for any major change in police power and fiscal capacity. Thus tax rates, bond issues, structural changes, annexations and mergers, were

[3] For an extensive discussion of the underlying political norms and their translation into governmental rules, see Charles R. Adrian, *Governing Urban America,* Second Edition, New York: McGraw-Hill Book Company, 1961.

submitted to the voters. *Vox populi* was indeed interpreted as *vox Dei*—the voice of the people was considered to be the only legitimate voice where major change was concerned. Wherever a group of residents saw their common interest demanding it, a municipality could be created. It was extremely difficult to destroy the legal entity once it was created without the consent of the citizens, while formal change was almost impossible except by referendum.

This governmental response to social change was one typical of social organizations. Every effort was made to persist in the earlier patterns of behavior, for such patterns represented commitments for many persons. In the face of the astronomical increase in population, in social functions, in the scale of the total society, every effort was made to carry on local government business as usual. For upon the existing scheme of things rested the plans and hopes of political bosses, ward heelers, contractors, private businessmen, ethnic enclaves—all those concerned with the city government as a major factor in their lives and business.

The emphasis during the period of rapid urbanization was upon getting the job done. If the city needed a streetcar grid, or a rapid transit, and the unwieldy city council objected, bribe the council. If the electoral machinery with its laundry list of elected officers made rational voting impossible, accept the organized machinery of the parties. If a hundred thousand new citizens did not understand Anglo-Saxon traditions of self rule let the "pols" teach them the ropes. It was a strategy of opportunism and expediency. In the process, the polity of the city was degraded; it became a necessary tool for the achievement of ends by private enterprise. The great capital investments of the period were largely the creation of private capital, working with franchises, contracts, and permits bought, stolen, or forced from the elected officials of local governments. When, in short, the burdens upon government became too much for the legitimate system of government, ways were found to circumvent the system.

HOW THE CITIES GREW UP

Needless to say, there was little concern for long-range planning in such a system. Government followed private enterprise: the labor force surged into a booming city, bringing its families and problems and social costs with it. Willy-nilly, government accepted the consequences—in the maintenance of public safety, the provision of charity, the extension of the city's physical plant, the policing of labor-management relations, the struggle to control organized criminal rings. Rather than planning for the future, urban government was continually struggling with its debts to the past, and it was always in arrears.

There was, after all, little to guide a planner. The fore-casting of urban growth is still a primitive science, and in the earlier days of urbanization when there was no precedent for such growth, nobody really understood what was happening. Thus the framework of local government was not radically reexamined in the light of the vast social transformation described earlier. Instead, reformers concentrated on the most obvious abuses in the existing system. They struggled to take the policy away from the political machines (those organizations interested primarily in the monetary rewards of politics) through the institution of nonpartisan government, civil service systems, and eventually the city manager form of government. The reformers were, in short, chiefly concerned with civilizing a governmental jungle where politics was simply a form of private enterprise.

However, the city was already changing under their feet, and with its change new problems emerged. The commuter trains, and later the electric railways, opened many new sites for settlement, some of them far beyond the city limits. Those with the resources in money and time began to move outward from the central city. The suburban dispersal had begun. As they moved outside city boundaries, the resources of the central city were no longer at their disposal. The suburban enclaves were faced with the house-keeping problems of the spatial community; under the permissive constitutional provisions, they solved them through incorporating their residential neighborhoods as villages or towns. Thus the central cities began to be surrounded by a series of satellites, incorporated and protected by governmental walls.

For a time the satellites did not constitute a problem. When the boundaries of the central city nudged those of the suburb, the suburb was annexed with little difficulty. However, such annexation came to a halt in the 1920's. Since that period most metropolitan areas have presented the same picture: a "land-locked" central city, increasingly aged and obsolete, surrounded by a growing patchwork of suburban municipalities. The key question is this: why did the boundaries of the central city cease to expand, following its dispersed population? We cannot answer with certainty; however, a comparison of central city and suburban population may be helpful.

Central City versus Suburbs

It was in the 1920's that the automobile revolution began to make vast areas on the outskirts of the cities available for residential sites. Country towns became nuclei for white-collar commuter settlements: empty pastures and cornfields became the sites for large scale housing development. But the people who left the central city for the suburbs were not a random assortment. As we have seen they were distinguished from those who remained behind by social rank, ethnicity, and life-style.

The automobile was at first used mostly by the upper social ranks. Its costs were substantial. Those who could bear these costs were also persons likely to want new residences, and new construction was largely on the periphery of the city. The older central city, with its structures dating back to the Age of Steam, had little space to offer those in search of new sites, but on the outskirts the supply was greater than the demand. There were, thus, powerful economic arguments for the location of new middle-class neighborhoods in the suburbs. With their construction, however, the physical difference between the two parts of the metropolis was augmented. The suburbs were new, middle-class, residential neighborhoods: the inner city was a mixture of workplace, markets and homes, surrounded by mile upon mile of older neighborhoods.

The new suburbs were also apt to be "exclusive." That is, they exercised formal and informal controls to prevent the "wrong kind of people" from moving in. Ethnic minorities, the foreign-born, Jewish, Catholic, or nonwhite citizens of the metropolis found the governmental walls of the suburbs impossible to scale. They perforce remained behind in the central city. Thus, with continuing in-migration of Negroes, Puerto Ricans, and Mexicans, the central city became ever darker in complexion, while the suburbs looked ever more "lily white" in contrast. The suburbs are, today, overwhelmingly populated by the white (or as Kipling called them, the "pinko grey") urbanites, usually a generation or more removed from the original immigrants. Most identifiable minority groups still live in the older central city.

We have noted earlier the increasing choice in life-style available to urban Americans. That kind of life which we have called familism, dedicated to children, home, and neighborhood, is best carried on in areas populated by similar people. In America, those who choose familism have a strong prejudice for the single-family dwelling unit secure in the middle of its fifty foot lot. Neighborhoods made up of such dwellings demand a great deal of horizontal space, space not to be found in the old central city without expensive demolition and rebuilding. With the automobile revolution, however, enormous new spaces became available on the outskirts. The suburbs attracted a population emphatically biased towards the familistic life-style, rather than the more unbane existence of the apartment houses in the densely developed center.

DIFFERENCE IN PEOPLE AND DIFFERENCE IN GOVERNMENT

Suburban folk tend to be of higher social rank, of white "old American" heritage, and committed to a familistic way of life. Though much of the city population is similar, much of it is different indeed. The older dwellings house a working-class population. The ethnic minorities, particularly the nonwhite enclaves, populate broad expanses of the city's housing grid. Those with a more urbane life-style remain in the city (and sneer at suburbia), while those committed to familism live in the outer wards of the city, or wait for the day when they can afford a suburban ranch house.

Such variation produces a lurid ideology—"the city is old and overrun by Negroes; the suburbs are shallow, jerry-built, cheap." This is reinforced by the governmental variation between the areas—"central city government is crooked; suburban government is trivial." The central city is one massive governmental unit, while the suburbs contain hundreds of little municipalities, with over 1,400 local units in the New York metropolitan area alone. Government in the city is big government. It represents a great deal of power, money, and technology, and it seems far away and hard to understand. It is also partisan government. In the suburbs the small municipalities are usually nonpartisan, and the white middle class feels that it has solved the problem of local government by taking politics out of government. In short, there are weighty differences between suburbs and central city with respect to physical plant, population types, governmental structure, and the political process. We will discuss the latter items in more detail; it is sufficient for the moment to indicate the very real differences between the two halves of the metropolitan complex.

The suburban municipalities are going concerns. Though they are small and weak, compared to the colossus at the center, most of them provide basic governmental services, collect taxes, and exercise the police power. Most important of all, they exercise a monopoly on the powers of municipal government as defined by the constitutional government of the states. While they hold such powers no other government can do so. And this is not unrelated to their reason for being.

THE ORIGINS OF SUBURBAN MUNICIPALITIES

Many of the early suburbs were collective responses to the problems created by interdependence. Small residential enclaves built their own power plants, sewers, water systems, because they could not share those of the central city and could not interest private enterprise in the job. Many of them were also incorporated to allow for a tighter control over land-use development and population than was possible for unincorporated neighborhoods. But recently, many suburban municipalities have one major purpose for their citizens: incorporation protects the residential community from annexation and governmental control by a larger unit. They are, in effect, governmental game preserves whose citizens are relatively immune to municipal law. Some suburban municipalities are simply industrial sites, freed from municipal smoke control and other nuisances; some are tax-free preserves for industry; some protect their citizens from adequate taxes and from housing codes, allowing them to build shanty towns, to keep chickens and cows, or to carry on home crafts and the like on rutty lanes without fire protection; some are governmental shelters where gambling, prostitution and other generally illicit activities are permitted.

In short, the Jacksonian ideology, appropriate enough to an agrarian society, produces a paradoxical governmental structure in the metropolis. It is free enterprise in the founding of governments, and every municipality for itself. The ease of incorporation allows for a multiplicity of municipalities, created for the most diverse purposes. (Many towns in Dade County, Florida, were incorporated for the sole purpose of securing liquor licenses; a state law allowed only two to a municipality.) All of these municipalities, once in being, constitute the *only* legitimate delegates of municipal powers. With respect to any larger problem or purpose, they are "dog in the manger" governments; they will not act, nor allow other governments to do so.

Any governmental entity, once in being, is difficult to disband. This is particularly true of the suburban municipality. The Jacksonian ideology supports rule by friends and neighbors, nurturing suspicion of the Big City. Whatever the truth, it flatters the citizens with an image of their community as a semi-rural small town, a repository of the rustic virtues. And, translated into the constitution of the state, the Jacksonian ideology requires popular consent for the extermination of any municipality. When campaigns occur to abolish, annex, or amalgamate such governments, however, all who think they benefit from the *status quo* are vocally opposed. Any existing structure builds up some differentially distributed advantages—somebody prefers it to alternatives. When this is combined with the poetry of

---

[4] For a lively picture of the changing American picture of the city, see Anselm Strauss, *Images of the American City*, New York: The Free Press of Glencoe, Inc., 1961

rusticity, the staying power of the municipality is clear. Thus the Dade County suburb, originally incorporated for the purpose of securing two liquor licenses, today stands for home, mother, democracy, and virtue. The imaginary boundary lines and the place name become symbols, made to contain the diverse values of the residential neighborhoods.

The Governmental Dichotomy and Some Consequences

Today, a bird's eye view of the metropolitan governmental structure would typically encompass the great circle of the central city and the dozens or hundreds of small units clustered side by side on the outskirts. More literally, the central city would be marked by higher, denser structures, shelving downwards rapidly to the peripheries; the suburbs would be horizontal, dispersed, with perhaps one-fifth the population of the inner central city per square mile. From a bird's eye view we would also note that the air over suburbia is often filled with fumes and smoke from the center. The whole urban complex lies across one or two great watersheds, and streams flow across governmental boundaries, bearing effluvia from here to there. The flow of traffic also moves momentarily throughout the area, without regard to municipal boundaries, knitting together the scattered sites for human activity in a larger system of action. In short, one would see the governmental division as arbitrary with respect to many of the collective systems of human action which constitute the being of the city.

Indeed, the entire urban complex is in many ways a unity. The scattered thousands are interdependent in each of the ways we have detailed; they man the complex, exclusive work organization we have discussed earlier. The wealthy suburbanites depend upon the unskilled ethnic laborers and machine operatives of the central city for the social product that feeds them. The central city banks depend upon the suburban investors; the suburban department stores depend on the central city banks. All of the residents together are subject to the age-old kinds of interdependence detailed earlier: they require order in intergroup relations, protection of person and property, and the maintenance of a transport system, water and sewage systems, fire protection and public health. In short, there is a sense in which we can call the metropolitan area a unity.

This unity, however, is not reflected in government. The problems created by contiguity and mutual dependence are not allocated to any government which includes all of those affected and affecting others. The central city government does not work in close cooperation with those of suburbia; how could it? Suburban governments are themselves uncoordinated, with no center of power and information. Yet the cooperation of suburbia is frequently crucial to the programs in the central city: traffic on a freeway system which ends abruptly in the main street of a country town is apt to back up halfway to City Hall, and smoke abatement will be less than complete until the suburban industrial park complies. There is, however, no normative prescription in Jacksonian philosophy for the forced integration of local government. Nor is there a constitutional formula that frees the governmental structure from the heavy hand of the referendum voter. Thus many important problems generated in the metropolitan complex are insoluble within the existing governmental structures. Our political culture lags far behind the emerging problems of the metropolitan world in which we live. It is embedded in the folk thought of the citizen and the phrases of the law.

SOME AUGURIES AND A QUESTION

Meanwhile, massive changes continue. In two decades our cities will grow by more than fifty million people. Most of the net growth will be in suburbia.[5] Even today, 49 per cent of our total metropolitan population lives in the suburban fringe. Thus the one large-scale government in the metropolis, that of the central city, will encompass a dwindling proportion of the land in use and the people in residence. There is little indication that the manufacture of small municipalities in suburbia will cease. While the scale of organization in the United States progressively increases, while work, play, religion, and other major activities are carried out through very large-scale organizational networks, local government moves doggedly in the opposite direction. Our ability to plan and provide for the entire metropolitan complex within the inherited framework of local self-government is declining relative to our ability to exercise over-all control in other segments of our lives.

Yet certain problems are inescapable. We refer, once again, to the minimal needs of human collectives living in cities. These problems are so basic that, should they not be solved, the city would perish. But our cities do not appear to be in such mortal danger, so we must ask: how is the polity maintained so that the resources and order requisite for these millions may indeed be predictably there when they need them? In answering this question, we shall consider first the government of the old central cities. Then we shall turn to the congeries of municipalities on the fringe, that dark and unknown governmental realm called suburbia.

Suggested Readings

On The Governmental Mosaic of the Metropolis

Exploring the Metropolitan Community, John C. Bollens, editor, Berkeley and Los Angeles: University of California Press, 1961.

[5] See Philip Hauser, *Population Perspectives*, New Brunswick, N.J.: Rutgers University Press, 1960, Chapter 4, p. 101.

This is the report of a large-scale study of metropolitan governments as they relate to each other and to the socio-economic structure of the urban settlement. Written in the context of a duty to recommend needed changes in the governmental structure of metropolitan St. Louis, it has the double aim of describing what is and prescribing what might be. Sample surveys of the citizens deal with their political participation and their opinions of their governments.

"Local Government Organization in Metropolitan Areas," Victor Jones, in Coleman Woodbury, editor, *The Future of Cities and Urban Redevelopment*, Chicago: University of Chicago Press, 1953. A detailed descriptive survey of the metropolitan governmental structures, with a discussion of the origins and effects of a fragmented local government. The collection in which this occurs is also a valuable source of information on the problems involved in "redeveloping" our cities.

On the Governmental Dichotomy and Some Consequences

"Metropolis in Ferment," *Annals of the American Academy of Political and Social Sciences*, 314 (November, 1957.) This entire issue of the *Annals* is devoted to the problems and prospects of the metropolis, and a great deal of attention is focused upon the results of the dichotomy between central city and suburbs.

4

The Governance of the
Central City

The aged central city, its structure reflecting the paleo-technic city of the nineteenth century, is the living past of the metropolitan area. Here we find the monuments to earlier technology, leaders, social circles, artistic achievement. Here the visitor feels that he has really discovered the essence of the metropolis. At Times Square in New York, the Loop in Chicago, Penn Center in Philadelphia, or Market Street in San Francisco the metropolis seems to come into focus. However, what was basic and definitive in an earlier city may be very misleading in a metropolis with half or two-thirds of its population living in the suburbs; the focus is far off center. Still there was a time not long ago when the central city did encompass the totality of the urban complex, and its downtown was the hub of the metropolis. Its governmental boundaries encircled the densely built-up urban area, and its polity was the public decision making process for the entire urban complex.

Before the automobile the central city included the entire

array and variety of the urban worlds. It took the brunt
of the rapid urbanization we have discussed; here was the
process of increasing scale in concrete form. The soaring
skyscrapers represented the "peak organizations" which
were melding continental networks of activity. Railroads,
banks, insurance companies, petroleum companies, all
built their headquarters at the center. One saw also the
other aspects of increasing scale—in the polyglot crowds of
Sicilians, Poles, Hungarians, and Jews who crowded the
streets of the lower East Side of Manhattan, the near North
or near South Side of Chicago. Areas of cheap, dense housing
lay close to the workplaces of the center and were the
typical ports of entry for the immigrants and country boys
drawn by economic opportunity and glamour to the city.

As we have noted, the government of the central city
faced a congeries of tremendous tasks. Increasing scale
produced new problems of intergroup relations. Expanding
economic enterprises, based on new energy sources and
machinery, were violent and radical departures from an
older organization of work. Labor agitation and labor
unions arose as a response to catastrophic change, from
a workforce still oriented to small-scale family enterprises,
shops and farms and crafts.[1] The relationships between
organizing labor and management were uneasy, unstable,
and frequently bloody from the Civil War to the 1940's
(and still are in regions of rapidly increasing scale, such
as the South). The government of the city was usually the
only agency responsible for maintaining public order
among these forces. At the same time, the sheer mixture
of populations produced endemic and violent conflict between ethnic enclaves. Negroes and Irish, Italians and
Jews, Poles and Negroes competed for homes, neighborhoods, jobs—living space. Their competition frequently
descended into overt conflict, and many of them did not
understand the "rules of the road" in an urban place

[1] For an organizational analysis of the rise of the labor unions, see
Scott Greer, *Social Organization,* New York: Random House, 1955.

ordered by the inherited laws of the Anglo-Saxon people. Small nuances of expression and tone of voice could turn a policeman's friendly admonition to, for example, a newly arrived Pole into a brawl or a murder.

The variation in cultural background alone produced great areas of anarchy and danger in the organizational interstices. The cities of America have old histories of rioting, lynching, and pillaging. In the streets, alleys, parks, lobbies, terminals, and public transport there were always problems of policing. The need for police always outran the supply, for the consequences of increase in scale to the local community were typically disregarded or underestimated. Weakness of the law enforcement agencies led, in turn, to the organization of effective criminal gangs. The wide array of illegal behavior, the variety of cultural backgrounds, and the poor control system meant that fortunes could be made in gambling, prostitution, and the sale of narcotics. The organizations that carried on such illegal commerce were frequently of different ethnic origins; thus gang warfare was both pecuniary and ethnic in its nature.

The development of the physical plant also lagged behind demand. Only in the twentieth century did most American cities assure themselves of a safe water supply. Streets and streetlights, sidewalks and their maintenance, continually demanded new outputs of societal wealth. Sewage disposal was a continual problem. Only extreme failure of the system made most citizens aware of its importance, yet sewage disposal systems had to expand continually because of the mushrooming population. We have not mentioned schools, parks, museums, libraries: all were in short supply as the customers multiplied astronomically.

The solution of these problems had to be found, as we have observed, within the framework of a democratic dogma. Vast and difficult operations were to be commanded by any "common man" who could be elected by the votes of others; important operating decisions were to be made by the voters in referendum elections. The moral and technical control of the government depended in large part upon the judgment of the ordinary citizen. But these citizens were frequently unable to understand even the English language, much less the complex system of American local government. Those who did understand were not competent to monitor the unprecedented process of city building and organization forced upon them by large-scale society in expansion.

ECONOMICS OF MACHINE GOVERNMENT

The impasse was resolved by the development of powerful party machines at the local level. The party machine was an organization devoted to the control of the vote and, through the vote, power and the profits of power. Without a guiding ideology (or set of formulated ideals) it operated as an exchange system, a business enterprise. At the lowest level the precinct captains exchanged jobs, bonuses, turkeys on Thanksgiving, coal in winter time, for the votes of families, friendship cliques, ethnic enclaves. The machine was a vast retail system for trade in votes. Frequently, of course, the actual voting could be made irrelevant, for fraud was another means of affecting the tally (which in turn affected the supply of "Wholesale goods" or authority to be exchanged). Plunkitt describes the hardship of his early days, when his wife stayed up all night ironing out ballots so that they might be inserted through the crack in the bottom of the ballot box. Without extensive discussion of the technology of fraud, let us note that the exchange of favors for votes was the staple technique, with fraud a supplementary device. Together, these allowed the machine to count on a dependable plurality. Of course, there are usually two or more party machines in competition. This fact introduced the note of uncertainty which heated up the campaign and made politics a great spectator sport in the nineteenth century cities.

The dominant machine was related to the rest of the

urban community through an exchange system. At the higher level, the political Boss treated with the financial and industrial interests of the city. His trading cards were franchises for the rapidly expanding transportation system, contracts for lucrative public works, permits to operate various businesses, as well as waivers of the public law for favored parties. His price was reciprocal favor or cash. Money, in turn, was reinvested in the machine, trickling down through district and ward to the precinct, where the precinct officers in turn distributed favors. (Of course, the Boss took substantial profits from the transaction.)

The importance of the cash nexus, and the relative public irresponsibility of the political Boss, meant that money could be translated into political power. Lincoln Steffens described, in some detail, the things that rich and respectable entrepreneurs bought from local government in the nineteenth century American city.[2] They were worth having. (A slightly fictionalized biography of Yerkes, the "Robber Baron" who bought the right to monopolize public transport in Chicago, is given in Theodore Dreiser's novel, *The Titan*.) Aside from using money, the upper class could also influence the local boss through the crusading daily newspapers (which might expose delicate and secret operations) and through power at the state or national governmental levels. In summary, there were many ways for business interests to determine policy in the city.

It was indeed a society oriented toward business. Businessmen were the first-class citizens, and the chief operations of government were delegated through contracts to business enterprise. The material tasks of local government, apart from such unprofitable enterprises as police and fire protection, were very small operations compared with the developing corporations of nineteenth century America. Though a majority of the citizens may have been ethnic

---

[2] *The Autobiography of Lincoln Steffens,* New York: Harcourt, Brace and Company, 1931.

and working class (in 1910 a majority of Americans were from minority groups), their interests were not paramount. Those of business were.

Such a system could be imagined as a pyramid, with a power elite at the top. The power elite was made up of the wealthy, whose control of men and money, whose ties with the national and state governments, whose influence with the newspapers, and whose "ownership" of the mayor and council (through the Boss) gave them tremendous leverage for the control of both the public and private aspects of the city's development. Such an interpretation was documented in dozens of novels; it was congruent with the stories of the muckrakers, as well as the ideology of the socialists, anarchists, and syndicalists. It was a conspiracy as local government, with politicians seen as merely tools of "the executive committee of the bourgeoisie."

THE POWER ELITE OF THE CITY TODAY

This image of urban government has persisted into our own day. Floyd Hunter has spent a great deal of energy identifying the "thirty men who run Atlanta."[3] Other scholars have studied a number of American cities. In each case they move from expert informants, who know the situation, to a set of nominated power figures. These in turn nominate others until the circle is closed and new persons do not get mentioned; from those most frequently nominated they select the personnel for the power elite.

Their technique has recently been radically questioned. Some have noted that, if there is only a *myth* about a power elite and it is believed by the more informed citizens, then the scholar is only documenting that myth when he asks them how they think the city works. This would explain

[3] *Community Power Structure,* Chapel Hill: University of North Carolina Press, 1953.

why we could find a power elite whether it exists or not. Others have more drastic criticisms. They note that when the "Big Mules" of Cleveland or St. Louis try to help reorganize the local government of the metropolis their projects go down in defeat at the polls. When the civic leaders of Chicago want to refurbish the near North Side, or locate a new campus for the University of Illinois, their efforts are frustrated and the final decision is made by the Mayor—or no decision at all results.[4] In short, the power elite image of control in the central city has lately been exposed to an extremely sceptical group of critics. This leads us to ask: Was the political image of the city equally fictitious in earlier days? Or do the critics of the power elite theory today simply misunderstand the nature of organization in the contemporary central city? It seems more likely that the discrepancy does not just reflect variation in opinion but instead indicates differences among cities and, more important, the continuing effects of increase in scale which change cities over time. The big city machine, a response to increase in scale, may also have become a victim of the continuing process. Let us look at urban government in this context.

Social Change and the Machine

Continual increase in scale has had four major consequences for the problems of urban government and their solution. It has produced an increasing bureaucratization of governmental and other functions: it has led to rapid organizational mergers in private enterprise; it has radically changed the general character of the urban population; and it has resulted in a massive multiplication of the popula-

---

[4] For a careful study of the way major issues of Chicago were resolved (or, more often, tabled) see Edward C. Banfield, *Political Influence*, New York: The Free Press of Glencoe, Inc., 1961.

tion and therefore of the size of the organizational tools of urban government. Let us consider each of these in relation to its implications for the classic big city machine.

The bureaucratization of governmental services affected the machine in two separate ways. First, with the Great Depression of the 1930's it became apparent that all Americans were part of a nationwide economic system, and when that system failed the problem of unemployment and poverty was a nationwide problem. As a consequence, what had been charity became the work of the Department of Health, Education, and Welfare, and vast programs were administered through the nationwide bureaucracies of government. Second, the management of local governmental enterprises became increasingly professionalized; the reformers were successful in convincing the people (and later the politicians) that such services as the city provided were better handled by civil servants, selected and trained through nonpolitical methods to do their jobs without favoritism or political counsel. These two changes struck deep at the roots of politics as a simple exchange system. The goods which the precinct captain once traded for votes were disbursed by a federal agency staffed by civil servants. The decisions about street layouts, hospital construction, zoning, and planning, once so profitably controlled by politicians, were increasingly made by professional public personnel—planners, hospital administrators, traffic engineers. At the same time voting became better organized, and mechanized, with a bureaucracy (subject to review) in charge of the tallies. Quality control made fraud difficult and dangerous. Both at the lowest and highest levels the exchange system of the machine was mortally damaged.

CORPORATE MERGER AND LOCAL POLITICS

The rapid and continuous process of organizational merger had other effects upon the urban polity. The drawing of major enterprise into national organizations and the further bureaucratization of the corporation, as it separated ownership from management, resulted in a class of professional managers whose first duty was to the nationwide, or international, corporate network. The most powerful economic figure in town was no longer the owner of the major industry; he was a manager. Consequently, the economic dominants (as they are sometimes called in the literature on the power elite) became increasingly withdrawn from concern with the local community. Schulze has documented the steps by which Ypsilanti, Michigan, moved from a classical power elite structure to one in which the branch plant managers were interested in the local community only on rare occasions. Rather than wishing to run the show, they only wanted a veto on certain kinds of governmental act. Otherwise, they did not wish to be involved.[5]

The result of corporate merger has been the freeing of economic organizations from dependence upon, and hence interest in, particular cities. This has combined with the increasing geographical mobility of the managerial elite; as they move upward in the corporate hierarchy they move around the country. They become identified with one community only when they have ceased to be occupationally mobile. (One longitudinal study indicated that, even in Red Wing, Minnesota, a town of ten thousand, the personnel change among those nominated as civic leaders was more than 60 per cent in the relatively short period of six years.)[6] Turnover of leadership makes effective organization (the compromising of interests, the assignment of tasks, the integrating of action) extremely difficult. Furthermore, we must remember that the business leadership in a city of

[5] Robert O. Schulze, "The Bifurcation of Power in a Satellite City," in Morris Janowitz, editor, *Community Political Systems*, Glencoe, Ill.: The Free Press of Glencoe, Inc., 1961.

[6] "Organizational Leadership and Social Structure in a Small City," Donald W. Olmsted, *American Sociological Review*, Vol. 19, pp. 273–281.

any size is apt to be divisible on more issues than those on which it is unitable. (A recent study by Scoble, for example, shows a very low rate of consensus among the dominant leaders in a New England town of less than fifteen thousand persons.) [7] It requires *more* work to achieve coordination when there is high turnover, yet there are fewer people committed to achieving it. In short, the changing nature of exclusive, membership organizations has greatly weakened their machinery for controlling the political decisions of the city. And such change is of particular importance in the metropolis, the headquarters city of the corporation.

POPULATION CHANGE AND THE MACHINE

Meanwhile, the population of the metropolis has been changing in the directions discussed earlier. Social rank has on the average moved upwards; the illiterate, unskilled workman of foreign birth is a vanishing breed. Even in the central city education, occupation, and real income have risen to once-unimaginable levels in the past sixty years. At the same time, the children and grandchildren of the foreign born are socialized from the beginning to the American urban milieu. As a result of these changes in combination the definition of the vote has changed; it is no longer simply an expression of ethnic solidarity, but rather a more complex decision, based on a variety of interests. The children of the immigrants live in a different city from that of their parents and have different techniques for managing their urban environment. Their toleration for fraud shrinks as they become more informed and committed to American civic virtues. Their vote is not for sale.

[7] "Leadership Hierarchies and Political Issues in a New England Town," by Harry Scoble, in *Community Political Systems*, Morris Janowitz, editor, Glencoe, Ill.: The Free Press of Glencoe, Inc., 1961.

An indirect effect of increasing size, but an important one, is the suburban-central city dichotomy. With increasing population and static boundary lines, the population of the metropolis is almost equally divided between central city and suburbs. But we have also noted the difference between the population in the two areas: those who remain in the central city are predominantly ethnic and working class social types. In 1950, according to Philip Hauser, "Los Angeles was the only city among the five largest in the United States in which the native white population of native parentage was greater than half, and even there it was only 55 per cent.[8] These populations are the ones most likely to prefer the Democratic party in national elections; when there is a partisan organization of local elections (and this is true of all but one of our very large cities) the working class and the ethnic voters go Democratic. A direct consequence is the collapse of the Republican Party in the political arena of the central city. One by one, Republican strongholds are giving way to Democratic majorities, as the nordic white Protestant middle class makes its way to the suburbs. Today, in many of our great cities, two or three Republican councilmen represent the "two party system" among a host of Democratic officials. As the process of segregation by polity continues, the central city will become, in fact if not in theory, a one-party state.

GROWTH OF THE GIANT BUREAUCRACIES

Finally, we have to consider the increase in the size of urban concentrations. In 1900 two American metropolitan areas had a population of a million or more; in 1960, there were nineteen complexes this large. The sheer aggregation of population had two major effects upon the control sys-

[8] Hauser, *Population Perspectives,* New Brunswick, N.J.: Rutgers University Press, 1960, p. 125.

tem of the central city. First, and not to be overlooked, was the sheer increase in the size of the problems that had to be handled within the rounds of urban housekeeping, and the consequent size of the organizations which handled them. The City of New York, for example, employs 50,000 persons in its educational system, 26,000 in its police department, and 13,000 in its fire department.[9] The sheer aggregation of numbers and budget results in the proliferation of organizational centers with a degree of autonomy and, hence, power. The number and strength of leadership groups is multiplied with increasing population.

The total effect of these changes has been the destruction of the old-time political machine, and with it the power elite. Increase in scale has destroyed the basis for the political machine *as an exchange system;* in the urban wards of Stackton it is as hard to recruit precinct workers as in the small-town Republican strongholds of Illinois. Whyte reports the visible attrition of the Democratic machine in Boston during the 1930's, while Reichley discusses the steady weakening of Republican power in Philadelphia during the same period.[10] The ability of the political boss to control his "Hessians" and through them the vote of the people, may have been over-rated in the past: it is very easy to over-rate it today.

The collapse of the exchange system has, in turn, destroyed the ability of the power elite to call the tune.

[9] Wallace S. Sayre and Herbert Kaufman, *Governing New York,* New York: The Russell Sage Foundation, 1960.

[10] The political machine in Stackton is described and analyzed by Peter H. Rossi and Phillips Cutright in "The Impact of Party Organization in an Industrial Setting," in Morris Janowitz, editor, *Community Political Systems,* Glencoe, Ill.: The Free Press of Glencoe, Inc., 1961. For the Philadelphia case see James Reichley, *The Art of Government,* New York: The Fund for the Republic, 1959. William Foote Whyte presents a study, in depth, of the changing relations of the machine to the ethnic neighborhood he studied in Boston, in *Streetcorner Society,* Chicago: University of Chicago Press, 1943.

Businessmen have never had a preponderant influence, at the polls, on the city population as a whole. They have relied upon the machine as a mechanism for translating money into political power. By bribing the politicians and by contributing to campaign chests, business interests assured themselves a strong voice in the political decisions of the central city. Even with the Republican Party's power fading away they could still exert leverage upon the Democratic machine, for the machine was primarily a non-ideological exchange system. With its weakening, however, the business man had literally no way of reaching the voters.

The result is a drastic separation of numbers and wealth in the contemporary metropolis. Businessmen, resident in the suburbs, have great stakes in the central city polity. That polity, however, is controlled by a set of politicians who have a declining need for the businessman, and who are elected by the votes of the ethnic and working class constituencies of the center. Such a separation of numbers and wealth is not, of course, contrary to the democratic dogma. It is, however, an anomaly to those who still consider the businessman as the first class citizen and his interests as paramount for the community.

It is also anomalous to those who explain American government through the theory of the two-party system, with its assumptions of organized control and competition for power. The anomaly leads us to ask: How, then, does the government of today's central city operate? How is it that order is maintained and essential tasks are performed?

The Machine of the Incumbents

The disappearance of party competition in the general elections of the central city does not destroy party organization. Instead it changes the basis of organization: the old-style exchange system is replaced by a new order. Before discussing the new state of things, however, it is important to note the cause and consequences of one-party government for the dominant Democratic organization.

The central city electorate, with its predisposition to vote Democratic, is (like the Southern Democrats) basically a captive electorate. Whoever is designated Democrat on the ballot will usually get a majority of the votes. One might jump to the conclusion that such one-party government could mean only a sort of totalitarianism. Instead, it seems to result in a general loosening of the control mechanism; as V. O. Key demonstrates for the one-party system in the South, the very basis for much of the party's control is weakened by the disappearance of the opposition party.[11] The reduction of threat in the general election eliminates the need for party discipline and ferocious *esprit de corps* for, no matter what happens, the Democratic Party will take most of the elective offices.

Under these circumstances, however, the Republican minority is rapidly demoralized. Political organization is postulated upon occasional victory; moral victories are sustaining only when there is some eventual possibility of non-moral, tangible victory. In the central city, however, Republican votes continue to decline despite all efforts made by the Republican Parties. As this occurs, the Republican Party's leadership and its elected local officials in cities like St. Louis and Chicago begin to resemble Republicans of the South. They are either lonely idealists, whose words are purely symbolic since they lack power to implement them, or else a sort of auxiliary of the dominant Democrats. (Chicago's delegation to the State legislature in Springfield includes the "sanitary Republicans," Republican legislators whose chief source of income is office in the Democratic-controlled Chicago Sanitary District.) Such officials may even vote with the Democrats and against their fellow Republicans on crucial issues. Thus even if the

[11] V. O. Key, *Southern Politics*, New York: Alfred A. Knopf, 1949.

Republicans had a powerful issue, it is doubtful that the existing leadership could mobilize a campaign to exploit it. They stand not so much for an alternative governance as for the existing distribution of electoral strength in the central city; in fact, they depend upon it for their working conditions.

THE DISASTER OF TOTAL VICTORY

The Democratic monopoly of victory in the general election, however, means that the primary election becomes the major arena for gaining office. And at the primary level the party organization is considerably weakened, for nomination to office (tantamount to election) becomes an apple of discord thrown among the Democratic ranks. In some cities the party cannot officially designate a slate in the primary; even when it can, its decisions are basically divisive. There are many deserving party men, and little to prevent one from running from his district. If he has been an effective leader at the block and precinct level, he may very well win, for the mobilization of friends and neighbors can easily produce strong opposition to the organization's designated candidate. Since the candidates do not need actual logistic support in the general election (the simple party designation will usually suffice), the field is clear for "mavericks" to compete.

Yet the party organization can usually control most of the offices in the primary election. The reason for this is clear enough; the ordinary voter usually does not know or care enough about the primary to vote. Thus the organization, though it may control only a small percentage of the potential vote, can nevertheless swing the margin of victory to its candidate. This organizational level is considerably augmented in many cities by the organization's control of the electoral machinery. Efforts range from differential requirements for certification as a candidate, to the ignoring of irregularities in the campaign and the voting (though the latter practices are becoming increasingly dangerous for reasons noted earlier). We may surmise also that much of the power of the organization results from a simple misapprehension of its effective force by potential dissidents. The machine *was* all-powerful for many years in some of our cities; those interested in politics are differentially exposed to the organization. They may fear official disapproval, not just in the immediate election, but in the future. Even if the party machine's power is now a myth, myths may long outlive their factual base and have consequences.

Thus the organization maintains a continuing control, though not an ironclad one, over the distribution of offices. However, with the disappearance of effective opposition it no longer needs the money of the businessman to win its campaigns. Being able to win the general election in any event, the power relations between politician and business leader have shifted radically. The politician is clearly in the more advantageous position: he has the trading cards.

ONE-PARTY GOVERNMENT AND CONTROL OF THE MACHINE

There have also been radical changes within the dominant party's organization. With the weakening of the machine, the power relation between the nonelective party Boss and the elected officials reverses. First the elected mayor develop a considerable autonomy from the machine; standing above all other elected figures in the metropolis, his role is visible and his words are news. From the rostrum of office he tends to dominate the mass media, and through the media develops a powerful electoral attraction of his own. Then party ceases to be a differentiating label in the one-party central city; the major differentiator becomes incumbency. Those who are in office become *de facto* rulers of the party, for the party needs them more than they need its cohorts. They dispense the patronage and make the decisions.

Thus the central city mayor assumes a major if not dominating role in the *dramatis personae* of local politics. Other stellar roles include the head of the county government and perhaps the president of the council or board of aldermen. They also are familiar figures in the news, for they are elected officials with city-wide constituencies in image if not in fact. Along with them rise the managers of the great governmental bureaucracies, school superintendents, engineers, police commissioners, and the like. Such men, elected or appointed, stand for the expertise of their office, the legitimacy of the tasks which their bureaucracy performs, and the logistics of money and men. The dominant figures in central city politics tend to be the dominant officials of government; they constitute a "machine of the incumbents." No matter how they reached office in the first place, once there they are formidable forces.

The central city mayor can, indeed, become an enemy of his party's organization. Concerned with the entire city, he is sensitive to opinion in the middle class, familistic, outer wards of the city; his political score in the general elections depends upon his ability to carry these "good government" and "newspaper" wards. He responds to the criticism of the daily press and the statements of public leaders representing various interests: welfare, hospital, education, and the like. Though these interests cannot defeat him at the polls, he nevertheless engages in implicit bargaining with them, anticipating the effects of his words and actions on the newspapers, civic leaders, and hence, the outer wards. At the same time the central city mayor is the dominant public official for the entire metropolitan area. Insofar as there is a metropolitan community, he is its highest elected official. (In St. Louis, suburbanites and central city voters alike accorded the Mayor of the City more trust and confidence than all other leaders combined, and their reasons rested upon his office, his expertise, and his character as a civic notable.) As representative of more than the laundry list of special interests in the area, he stands for the general welfare. Businessmen, no longer his employers, return as influentials insofar as they are virtual representatives of many values and aspects of the metropolis.

In fact, the central city mayor tends to believe that good government is good politics. But in the process of pursuing good government he may destroy much of the effectiveness of the Democratic organization.[12] The separation of the offices of precinct captain for the party and precinct captain of police may be good governmental administration: it may also be very demoralizing for the political actors who had counted upon the promotion to police captain as a possible reward. Nevertheless, the metropolitan mayor is free to continue his swing towards good government, for the machine cannot control him. And he may look beyond the central city, to position in the state government, or the federal government in Washington, where his "good government" policies may count heavily. Furthermore, he is, ironically, strengthened at home by his symbolic separation from the machine. He can have his cake and eat it too. Meanwhile the old-style political machine is further weakened; the rewards of political work disappear right and left. As one consequence, the persons who can be recruited for the hard and tedious work at the block level change in character; the ranks of party workers become disproportionately composed of those who have few alternatives for social distinction and mobility. The over-all picture is one in which old-style machine politics fades away before the new order, the machine of the incumbents.

To repeat the argument: The continual segregation of

---

[12] Banfield discusses the destructive effect of the "good government mayor" at some length in *Political Influence*, New York: The Free Press of Glencoe, Inc., 1961.

population by governmental boundaries means an increasing domination of the central city vote by the poor, the ethnics, and therefore the Democratic party label. This, in turn, relaxes the tensions of conflict at a party level, leading to a one-party state. To be sure, the process has gone further in some cities than others; it is still possible for the Republicans to win a battle occasionally if their wards are numerous and the Democrats make a series of catastrophic mistakes.

This will become rarer as the proportion of working class ethnics increases. It is also true that, in West Coast cities like Los Angeles, Republicans may rule under the guise of nonpartisanship. It is likely, however, that such cities, never having known a machine, have simply skipped a stage and landed directly in the future—the one party or non-party polity ruled by the machine of the incumbents.

The Weakening of Positive Government

One-party government, in fact, approaches very closely the condition of non-partisan government. The weakening of the party organization's hold on the incumbents softens the impact of those who wish to translate wealth and social power garnered in other fields into pressure on the policy of the city. The incumbents are freed from many pressures; however, it is a "freedom from," rather than a freedom to accomplish new and radical enterprises. This is because power becomes basically fractionated and dispersed. The elected officials, the heads of the great bureaucracies, state and federal levels of government, private capital, and the party organization, each hold certain resources necessary for massive action. To these must be added the governmental divisions of the metropolis. Multiple municipalities, counties, and special districts are vested with the legitimate power to perform certain tasks and to refuse to cooperate in others.

Banfield's description of Chicago emphasizes the continual deadlocking of these forces. In *Political Influence* he notes that the political head (usually the mayor) will ratify almost any proposal on which principal parties can agree. He thus escapes criticism from newspapers, civic leaders, and the like. However, he hesitates to force compromise because of the cost in goodwill, support, public image, or other intangibles of influence. He can usually afford to wait indefinitely for decisions to emerge: what usually emerges is stalemate. Of the six major issues Banfield studied (all of the major public issues for a two year period), two were resolved, one was abandoned by its protagonists, and the remainder were simply tabled. Thus half the major public issues remained in limbo. This is hardly evidence of a tightly knit ruling clique. Instead, Banfield sees the power elite as essentially part of "The Mythology of Influence."

The notion that "top leaders" run the city is certainly not supported by the facts of the controversies described in this book. On the contrary, in these cases the richest men of Chicago are conspicuous by their absence. Lesser business figures appear, but they do not act concertedly: some of them are on every side of every issue. The most influential people are the managers of large organizations the maintenance of which is at stake, a few "civic leaders" whose judgment, negotiating skill, and disinterestedness are unusual and, above all, the chief elected officials. Businessmen exert influence (to the extent that they exercise it at all) not so much because they are rich or in a position to make threats and promises as, in the words of one of them, "by main force of being right."[13]

To be sure, Banfield thinks that if all the wealth were organized in a permanent organization, it could exert great influence on the polity. This is not likely to come about, however, for three reasons: (1) there are fundamental conflicts of interest among private organizations, (2) the required communication would be great enough to cut seriously into the time necessary for private interest, and

[13] *Ibid.*, p. 288.

(3) any formal organization would rapidly become immobilized by its own commitments and organizational structure.

The overriding power of the mayor is also a logical possibility in Banfield's interpretation. He dismisses it in these words.

> To be sure, his power is great enough, thanks to the machine and to his ability to make the trades the planners deplore, so that he can exercise wide discretion in almost any matter. But being able to exercise discretion in almost any matter does not mean that he can exercise it in *all* matters. With respect to any one or two, or any few, moves, he is free. But if he wishes to stay in the game and to win, most of his moves, like most of the moves of the "civic leaders" and the businessmen in *their* games, must be determined by the exigencies of the game itself. Like them, he must act as the game requires or else get out of it.[14]

Thus Banfield's picture of Chicago is one that underlines the stability of the order, its underlying resistance to change, and the recalcitrant nature of government as a tool for major control and planning.

Sayre and Kaufman come to similar conclusions with respect to the greatest city in the country, New York City. Much as they love it, they report that its government is essentially static and conservative. The council is hamstrung, the mayor has responsibilities far beyond his power, and the Board of Estimate (made up of borough presidents and some central city officials) has usurped effective power. The result is a city government which has no legislative process, no strong executive, no party division visible to the public: one which is, in short, neither democratically responsible nor capable of a strong polity. Neither innovation nor planning can come about except in piecemeal response to the maintenance needs of the great city bureaucracies whose managers are as important in New York as in Banfield's Chicago.[15] For the Mayor of New York to function as leader and responsible head of the govern-

---

[14] *Ibid.,* pp. 302–303.
[15] Sayre and Kaufman, *op. cit.,* Chapter XVII.

ment he must be a political genius. When any social role requires such a rare person to operate it, we can judge it poorly designed for a world dominated by the "fairly bright."

The mayors of our great cities, symbols and symbolic leaders of the metropolitan community, reign but do not rule. They are brokers, conciliators, who reconcile the people to what they get from their government. They legitimatize the *fait accompli* on the rare occasions when the necessary resources for action result from transitory coalitions among the major contending organizations. For the rest, they preside over routine caretaker governments. And from one point of view, this is what the situation may seem to demand. The pioneer work of building the plant and establishing an order for the central city is long since complete: the population explosion will not rock its foundations, for a vast apparatus is in existence, and new growth will largely settle outside the center, in suburbia. The great bureaucracies which provide necessary governmental goods and services are already in being: they pursue the organizational destiny of expansion, increasing professionalization and multiplying the career opportunities for civil servants. All this they can do within the precedents established in the past and legitimatized through use.

There is, however, no organization capable of mounting a major offensive for innovation. The central city's polity is passive and adaptive before the continuing results of increase in scale; only catastrophe seems capable of creating the opportunity for new development. Meanwhile, the trends continue; the suburban move of industry is added to the differentiation of central city and suburban populations, the increasingly obsolete neighborhoods, and the increasing proportion of colored populations who suffer most from economic depression and expect the most action from their city government. Taken all together these trends result in a rapid drift of the city away from its older status of centrality and totality. Faced with such changes, most people who consider the central city's destiny agree that massive counteraction, planning and construction, and governmental change are necessary. Such counteraction is difficult to imagine within the governmental structure of our great cities as they operate today.

Suggested Readings

On the Economics of the Machine and the Power Elite

Streetcorner Society, William Foote Whyte, Chicago: University of Chicago Press, 1943. A detailed and fascinating study of the relations between the political machine and the social structure of an Italian slum. This volume is already a classic, although there have been very few parallel efforts. This may be due to the decline of the machine protrayed here.

Political Influence, Edward C. Banfield, New York: The Free Press of Glencoe, Inc., 1961. A detailed study of the "power structure" of Chicago as it responded to the six major issues which arose over a two year period. Banfield's study is a test of the hierarchical image of local government; it is also a valuable documentation of the little wheels of decision-making which presumably make the bigger wheels work. His discussion of "The Mythology of Influence," Chapter 10, is particularly useful, as is his formulation of the political-economic problems to which machine government is one answer.

On Social Change and the Machine

The two works above are both valuable for this subject. In addition, *The Art of Government*, by James Reichley, New York: The Fund For the Republic, 1959, is a useful description of the processes by which the Republican machine in Philadelphia declined and was finally overthrown. Reichley's piece includes an interesting discussion of the likelihood that alternatives to machine government will develop.

On The Weakening of Positive Government

In addition to Banfield's work cited above, see Wallace S. Sayre and Herbert Kaufman, *Governing New York*, New York: The Russell Sage Foundation, 1960. This is an encyclopedic description of our largest urban government: the ossification of policy and dominance of bureaucracy are clear.

5

The Suburbs: "Republics in Miniature"

The concept of suburbia is a hazy one. It is one that changed through time, adding meaning indiscriminately, until today it can mean simply the outer edges, the residential spillover of the city, the little "bedroom community," the home of the organization man, the upper-class municipality, or the dead level of American middle-class society. Through time it has gathered symbolic overtones; it is a fighting word. Those who are still ambivalent about America's urbanization may value suburbs indiscriminately as the representatives of small town and rural values; those committed to an urban style of life may see them as only a movement backward, a regression to the "nuzzling herd society of the village." Obviously, a term so mixed in its reference must be clarified before it has any utility at all.

We can distinguish four kinds of meaning for the term.

First, and clearest, suburbs are urban areas outside the governmental boundaries of the central city; they may or may not be incorporated as municipalities. Second, any outlying district far from the center may be called suburban; this is the ecological or spatial meaning. Third, suburban population is frequently considered to have distinctive attributes: it is more familistic, of higher social rank, and less ethnic. Finally, many persons have imputed a particular kind of social structure to the suburbs; they are regions where the spatially based group, the community, is strong. Neighborliness, friendship among fellow residents, a proliferation of organizations in the area, are taken to be attributes of suburbanism as a way of life.

Because this is a book about government, we shall take the first meaning as definitive and relate it to the others. We are concerned with those urban populations that live outside the boundaries of the central city but are part of the urban whole through interdependence of the kinds discussed earlier. Looking at such populations *en masse,* we can make some generalizations. First, the central city's boundaries usually include populations nearest the center; suburban populations are apt to be more spatially isolated from the center. Second, suburban buildings, reflecting more recent construction, are apt to be suitable as new residences for population types that are on the increase, and to be inhabited by them. These are households of middle to upper social rank, generally native-born and white, and familistic in their life-style.

Their relative isolation from the ambit of the central city means that their daily experience does not center in the typical social groups of the center. Their lives, particularly if they are women and children, are bounded by the immediate residential community, the public schools, playgrounds, streets, and business centers of the peripheral settlement. Even men, though they work in the center, spend a majority of their time, and their freest time, in the home community. The assortment of similar people into given residential areas by social rank, life-style, and ethnicity means that the average suburban family lives among its own kind.

The homogeneous and familistic populations of suburbia produce a particular kind of associational structure. Bound together by the interaction of children, the similarity of family norms and family goals, and a common commitment to the neighborhood as the site for home and and family living, familistic populations develop intensive neighboring patterns. Out of their common interests in the school, the care of children, the maintenance of the residential values in the area they develop organizations to defend and promote those interests. The familistic neighborhoods manifest a high density of formal voluntary organizations—P.T.A., Boy Scouts, and other youth centered groups, fraternal and service organizations, community-oriented organizations, church-centered organizations. From the familistic nature of the population, in contiguity and interaction, results a powerful organizational structure. Based upon interdependence, it leads to communication, involvement, and the ordering of behavior. Suburban neighborhoods are more apt to approach the conditions of true "social community." This is what some of their incoming residents seek.

SUBURBS AND SUBURBS: VARIATIONS

The populations outside the political bounds of the central city, however, manifest considerable variation in all these attributes. Although most suburban areas are farther from the center than most neighborhoods of the center city, there are anomalies. Some incorporated municipalities have been enveloped by the central city, yet retain their independence. They are governmental islands surrounded by the sea of the central city. Here we find the industrial "shelters," governments used only to protect industry from regulation and taxation by the central city. Here also we find such persisting municipalities as Hamtramck in Detroit (a Polish neighborhood) and Culver City in Los Angeles. On the other hand, some central cities have far-flung boundaries and include in their limits residential areas which are fifteen miles or more from the center. Such neighborhoods are ecologically isolated, but integrated into the central city's jurisdiction.

We have already noted the fact that the central city contains many familistic neighborhoods. Suburbia also contains areas where the population is more urban than much of the central city, where ethnic populations are concentrated, and where social rank is very low. A result of historical patterns in land development, these variations indicate we must be careful of loose generalization. In the St. Louis metropolitan area, for example, one suburb (University City), though of higher social rank, is predominantly Jewish and more urbane than the average in its typical life-style. Another (Kinloch) is of extremely low social rank, entirely Negro in its population, and more familistic than the average for the central city Negro population. There are working-class suburbs in growing numbers as the automobile becomes a universal possession and new land is opened to settlement. And the older suburban populations nearest the central city boundary become increasingly urban in life-style when apartment houses, market centers, and manufacturing plants are located within their boundaries. (Satellite manufacturing cities like Gary, Indiana, are a somewhat different case; their population is seldom of the sort discussed above.)

Thus the governmental definition of suburbia does not exactly coincide with the ecological or the population-type definitions. Nevertheless, the picture that holds true on the average, the best possible summary, is this. Most suburbs are far from the center, separately incorporated settlements of familistic populations. Whether ethnic or not, whether high or low in social rank, their familistic life-styles produce the kind of social order sketched above. They are beehives of interaction at the neighborly level, and a large proportion of their households are members of local organizations, are involved in a spatially defined local community.

THE IDEAL SUBURBAN POLITY

These attributes have led some of us, as Wood notes, to see them as "the Republic in miniature," a site for the revival of Jeffersonian democracy.[1] Though the sturdy yeoman has been replaced by the husband who brings home the salary check from the central city, though the round of country life has diminished to the problems of caring for lawn and shrubbery and do-it-yourself construction in the backyard, though the dominant actors in community affairs may in fact be women, the suburban municipality is still conceived of as a stronghold of democratic government and society. What are the reasons for such beliefs?

First, the size of the suburban municipality approaches that of the small town and village. (The median size in St. Louis County is around one thousand; no suburban municipality was over sixty thousand in population.)[2] With smaller size goes a smaller scale in the political and governmental organization of the community. Giant bureaucracies with unknown heads give way to city departments with acquaintances at their head and city councils with friends among the incumbents. Second, the relative similarity of all the residents (a result of segregation and concentration by ethnicity, social rank, and life-style) results in common interests and ease of communication. Values in common and clearly understood norms allow a

[1] Robert Wood, *Suburbia, Its People and Their Politics,* Boston: Houghton Mifflin Company, 1959.
[2] *Exploring The Metropolitan Community,* edited by John Bollens, Berkeley and Los Angeles: University of California Press, 1961.

form of interaction we have called communion. The dense interactional system in the neighborhoods and the residential areas means that such values are communicated, celebrated, and become social fact.

At the same time, so the theory goes, government is closer to the people. They can see its actions, understand its operations, and monitor its consequences. It is accessible to all. The citizen communicates with his government directly, in the hearings of the city council, or indirectly, by his participation in local organizations which represent his interest before the governing bodies. His government is in turn exposed to the responses of the governed. These arguments for small local governmental units, of course, assume an entire theory of how government works today. Let us examine the results of one study bearing on the question.

In 1956-1957 a large-scale study of government in the St. Louis metropolitan area was focused on precisely such questions.[3] From a large sample survey of the suburban residents we can construct some tentative generalizations about the "republic in miniature." We shall concentrate upon the relationship between citizens and their governments, for this seems to be the crucial point.

The residents of suburban St. Louis County are not any more interested in their local elections than are those of the central city. In fact, they are slightly less likely to vote in municipal or school board elections. Nor do they rush to the stump and compete for office; in the municipal elections of 1957, the smaller the municipality the less likely were the prospects of competition for office. Among the smallest municipalities, in fact, there tended to be only one slate running, and in several villages *nobody* would run for office. (In these cases the hapless incumbents were

[3] *Ibid.* See the author's contribution, particularly Part III, "Citizen Participation and Attitudes," on which the following discussion is based.

forced, by law, to remain in office.) This political indifference might be attributed to satisfaction with government. However, it is important to note that a very large percentage of the suburban population did not even know that they were part of an electorate that voted on local officials. One-fifth of the suburbanites did not know that the people in their area could vote for municipal officials; nearly one-third did not know they voted for school board officers. (In the central city the proportions were dramatically lower, 5 per cent and 20 per cent.) In short, the political system of suburbia completely missed a large proportion of the residents.

This brings us to an important point, however. There is considerable variation among suburbanites in their relationship to both the social structure of their community and its political process. There are three distinct types of participation in the local society of suburbia; (1) Community Actors, who are involved in the larger local community, (2) Neighbors, who participate only in the small-scale world of the neighborhood, and (3) Isolates, who have no role in either kind of social structure.[4]

Community Actors are the key personnel of the suburban political community. They are consistently more informed and aware of public personages and issues, and they are very likely to vote in the local elections. Neighbors are much less likely to be either informed or involved, while Isolates are generally outside both the communication flow and the action that takes place on the local scene. About

[4] The theoretical derivation of this typology is presented in the author's article, "The Social Structure and Political Process of Suburbia" in *The American Sociological Review*, Vol. 24, pp. 514–526. Evidence supporting the importance of the types is presented in "The Social Structure and Political Process of Suburbia: An Empirical Test," in *Rural Sociology* (in press at this writing). An extensive discussion of the social structure of suburbia is found in *The Emerging City, Myth and Reality*, Scott Greer, New York: The Free Press of Glencoe, Inc., 1962.

four out of ten residents of the St. Louis County suburbs were Community Actors; nearly the same proportion were Isolates; the remainder were Neighbors. However, the local electorate is disproportionately composed of the Community Actors; 70 per cent of them vote in local elections (compared with about 30 per cent of the Isolates.) Thus the suburban electorate is apt to mirror the concerns of those most informed and involved.

With qualifications, then, we may accept some of the assumptions of "the republic in miniature." Community Actors are most common among the familistic populations and, though they are as likely to be among such populations in the central city, they are most likely to translate their community interest into political action in the suburban towns. Furthermore, familistic populations are more common in the suburbs, so there are many more Community Actors to draw from. Manning the civic "table of organization," very often constituting the decisive electoral force, these self-selected citizens of suburbia are virtual representatives for those who do not care enough to participate.

What kinds of public problems do these representatives face in their diminutive polities? What are the issues of suburban politics, and what are some mechanisms for their solution? To answer such questions we must return, again, to the broader problems of increase in scale and spatially based organization.

Political Issues of Suburbia

The rapid spread of suburban settlement is first of all a result of increase in societal scale. Many political issues of suburbia grow out of the various concomitants of increase in scale, developing out of the question: how can we organize to accommodate these changes? We emphasize two aspects of the former: (1) the sheer expansion of suburban settlements in a short period of time, and (2) the broader changes in the nature of the American population's way of life.

SUBURBAN COMMUNITY PROBLEMS

Rapid increase in population, in suburb after suburb, has automatically produced problems. First, there is the question of controlling new growth. What kinds of enterprise and population are wanted, and where should they be located? The commitments made in the present are the limits within which the future must work. Furthermore, simple increase in quantity inevitably means an expansion of the services and goods provided by the government. This brings up the entire question of equity: who shall pay for the new plant and its operations, and who shall benefit, and how shall these be related? Sheer expansion of residential numbers thus creates serious issues: equally serious are those created by change in way of life.

We have said that the entire population is experiencing changes, with movement upwards in social rank, with increasing familism, with rapid acculturation of many ethnics to the "all-American way of life." In the suburbs each may result in the creation of major public issues. Increasing social rank means a general rise in the level of living of the population; the streetcar rider as he grows older has two cars in his garage, the tenement dweller's children live in a ranch house with three bathrooms, and the grandchildren of the urban poor worry about their income taxes. As these citizens come to expect more and better privately purchased goods and services, they also expect more of their government. Thus, even if the suburban government approximates the consumption norms of yesterday, the rising aspiration of its residents may leave it continually in the red. Those once satisfied with gravel streets today object to paved four-lane roads because they are inadequate to the rush hour traffic. Septic tanks give way to costly sewerage disposal systems: the small schoolhouse becomes a sprawling campus within an educational system, and the pressure is on the superintendent to add classes for "exceptional children," to expand the school's medical program, to add more cultural and community functions. In many suburbs there is continual demand for increased park space, public swimming pools, and playgrounds. All of these services cost money, demand taxes, and raise the question: Can we afford it? How shall we pay for it?

The increasing investment of Americans in home and family also results in issues for suburban communities. With increasing commitment to it as a *home,* the suburban residential area stands for the future of an investment in property—its image, environment, market value. It also stands for the kind of life a person desires for his family. The neighbors are the most important social environment of the wife and children, and the public schools are in many respects the most crucial environment and resource for the children's later careers. The familistic populations are deeply invested in their neighborhoods, and through them their residential community; thus the political structure, which may influence all of these, is of major concern.

Finally, with the increasing acculturation of many ethnic minorities to the middle-class American way of life, some interesting and important issues arise. For the second generation Italian, Pole, or Jew a move into suburbia may be the most striking signal of success. For those who have arrived, however, it may be a signal that the neighborhood is being "invaded," that cherished values are threatened. And when the second generation has arrived in a suburb, what is it to think about the middle-class Negro family that wishes to move in? The still-swarthy second-generation Mexican-American clan? The acculturation of ethnics raises as many problems as their original encapsullation in the ghettos raised—and raises many of them in suburbia.

PROBLEMS INTO POLITICAL ISSUES

Translated into the political issues of suburbia, any of these changes may produce fierce debate and electoral struggle. First, and perhaps prior to any specific decision, is the general question: how shall the political order be drawn, so that it will satisfy the democratic dogma and at the same time create and maintain the kind of community desired? How shall the voters be organized, the key officials chosen, and what kind of power shall they have? Who shall be represented, and in what way? The range of solutions here is wide. Some suburbs operate with a one-party system, the "good government caucus," which hand-picks a slate for office. They may further avoid politics by leaving the day-to-day operation of government in the hands of a manager. Other suburbs, however, tend to divide into political moities: the "ins" and the "outs," the older residents and the newcomers. They may struggle for office, or may even struggle over the basic constitution of the city. (This may be a battle for a new city charter, or it may be focused upon changing the municipality's "class" and therefore governing forms according to the State constitution.) Such issues typically arise in periods of rapid change, when the municipality is new or when it has accepted a large number of new residents.

A second and continuing type of issue is that of service provision. What services and what levels of services should the municipal government provide? The possibilities are practically infinite, but the budget is always tight. When the service level is decided, the next question is: How shall we pay for them? How shall benefit and cost be related? Who shall decide? These questions range from the proper method of issuing bonds (what rate of discount, what period of time, renegotiable or not) to the proper method of assessing property for taxation. Such issues become salient whenever the consumption norms of the population have risen, or the existing level of services has declined (due to a shrinking tax base, inflation, or a flood of new residents).

A third congeries of issues is generated by commitment to the community. When this is combined with rapid growth in the suburban area, very serious conflict may arise. Planning and zoning issues may become battlegrounds for rival factions. Should Meadowlane become a partially industrial municipality, with many of the characteristics of the central city left behind? What of the increased traffic in trucks, the commuters from elsewhere who work in the plants and warehouses? Or, should the beaches of Winonama be opened to the public? What of the transients who will drop in, unknown and perhaps dangerous to the play of local children? Or, should a bowling alley be allowed on the corner of Elm and Aster? So near the school, and selling beer? (Though this latter sounds ridiculous, it was, in fact, taken seriously by the leaders of one suburban municipality.) In short, what kind of a community are we trying to build (or maintain) and how shall we go about doing it?

Closely related to the last type of issue is any matter having to do with schools. As we have stressed already, the familistic population of suburbia, with its concern for children and their future, is particularly conscious of the school system. (In the St. Louis area the *only* widespread concern for schools was among the higher rank, extremely familistic suburbs.) For one thing, most people in familistic neighborhoods have children in the public schools; for another, the school tax is ordinarily between half and three-fourths of the total local tax bill in suburbia. Thus a decision on school policy may easily become a major public issue. In one "blue ribbon" suburb, for example, increasing population forced the construction of another high school.

However, the existing school was a very famous one, generally agreed to be one of the best in the United States. The outcry over the new school was heart-rending, for as many parents whose children would attend the new high school said, "We moved here in the first place to give our children the benefit of going to X High School."

Finally, and again connected with the previous issues, we have the question of ethnicity. Who shall be accepted in this community which contains our treasures, home, family, children, and neighborhood? A recent and vivid example of such an issue was the action of the Village Council in Deerfield, Illinois. The council condemned a large plot of ground for a public park, shortly after the real estate development company that owned it announced that the residential neighborhood it was building would be integrated and one-fifth Negro. This case was lurid enough, and was widely publicized. Many other struggles go on "within the family" of the suburban town's population. The Jewish child who is the only one in his school room not invited to a birthday party; the Negro family which quietly sells its house after vandals have broken the windows, such incidents as these, while not overtly political in nature, indicate something about school integration and equal protection under the law in the suburban municipality. At the same time, we must remember that such issues can have opposite resolutions: many of our most exclusive residential suburbs have substantial Jewish and Catholic populations, and even Negroes are eventually accepted in some cases (and in small numbers).

In summary, most of the issues of suburban politics seem to center around a few questions. What is the most common image of the desirable community? How can it be created (or maintained)? What will be the price and who shall pay that price? In the community image are summarized the aspirations of middle-class, familistic, white citizens of native birth. There is a paucity of information on the political processes by which such decisions are made. In the next section, however, we shall try to learn something about suburban politics by examining some municipal systems.

Suburban Political Orders

A major characteristic of suburban politics is their non-partisan nature. The national Democratic and Republican Party organizations or labels are seldom important factors in the elections of the suburbs. It is tacitly agreed that "there is no Republican or Democratic way of collecting garbage," that the general interests of the community are the proper center of concern and are irrelevant to larger political issues. The politics of suburbia is a friends-and-neighbors politics, largely non-ideological in nature. Like the machine, it is little concerned with the long-run character and fate of the nation; its primary concern is with the building of neighborhood communities and the housekeeping tasks of the spatial area.

The disappearance of the party label, however, means that elected officials are largely middle-class Republicans. The basic dominance of business ideology, the businessman as first-class citizen, is sharply evident in suburbia. Thus in St. Louis County, in 1956, the largest single occupational category represented in elected municipal offices was that of manager and professional, employed by business firms outside the suburban municipality where office was held. The second most important category was that of local businessman or professional in the electing municipality. A majority of elected officials were from these categories. This reflected, of course, the general composition of the suburban residents—but it was far more than a proportional representation of these categories.

When the electorate is organized on a party basis, it is typically a local, municipal party, concerned only with local affairs. The independents, the Good Government

Party, the Progressive Party appear in many suburbs; they nominate slates and campaign for their election on purely local issues. The personnel of such parties reflects the social structure of suburbia; Community Actors are their basic cadres, and these actors are about equally made up of men (usually`absentee-employed) and their wives. Thus suburban local politics has a distinctly heterosexual flavor; women are probably better represented in the political process of suburbia than at any other level, anywhere else in America.

As we have noted earlier, there is considerable variety among suburban municipalities. Though most are familistic, some are working-class and some are "blue ribbon" suburbs of the wealthy; a small but growing proportion are urban and hardly distinguishable from the middle wards of the central city; a few are predominantly ethnic. Such variations are important for the political process of the community, but probably the most important variation of all is simply that of stability. Rapid change is typically the ground for the raising of serious questions which, translated into political issues, are fought out in the local arena. It sets clear and ineluctable tasks for the governmental process. So important is this dimension that we shall sketch in two suburban municipalities at the poles of stability and change. They are both in Cook County, Illinois; both are far above average in social rank; both are extremely familistic in average life-style. We shall label the changing community Upward Ho, and the stable one Valhalla.

UPWARD HO!

This town was for many years a country village on the outskirts of Chicago, the center of a market-gardening area. It was largely controlled by a country-town political organization, Democratic by allegiance, and closely tied in with the Cook County Democratic Party. Though a Republican organization also existed, it lost power steadily as the area slowly grew in population. On the whole, it was a rural version of typical Cook County politics.

After World War II, however, population flooded the site. The increase between 1945 and 1960 was well over 1,000 per cent, and is was largely from the central city of Chicago. It was also heavily Jewish. Upward Ho! became a suburb inhabited by second and third generation ethnics who were leaving the central city for the surburban neighborhoods, though the jobs which sustained them were still in the older areas. These new suburbanites were at first content to accept the old political order which ran the "village" (the village rapidly passed the ten, twenty, thirty, forty, and fifty thousand population marks). However, the newcomers began to define the older political order in terms reminiscent of their central city backgrounds; a study in 1958 indicated *one hundred per cent* agreement that Upward Ho! had a power structure, made up of one man! In other words, the head of the older organization was defined as a Boss.

The newcomers began slowly to organize. They did so because of a new and different image of the community and its proper political process. The issues which recurred with regularity centered around the land use of the municipality and the expansion of the school system. For them, both kinds of development should be subordinated to their own stake in a proper residential enclave; the location of industry and commerce, of roads and public improvements, should all be decided in terms of their effects upon existing neighborhoods. The older political order, however, had long been committed to mixed development, with large-scale industrial growth as the most lucrative investment of community land.

Thus, upon the concrete issues of land use and schools, and upon the constitutional issues of Boss rule and village government the newcomers organized to challenge the old order. In response, the old order achieved a degree of coherence; both Republican and Democratic organizations opposed the reform party. They also invented a "do gooder" name for their political front, and coopted a number of newcomers into their organization. The battle has see-sawed for a number of years, the superior organization and commitment of the old heads balanced by the amateur, good government appeal of their challengers. Without a doubt, it will continue in one guise or another for some time, as massive growth continues to create new public issues with every election. The two-party system, once in existence, is a useful mechanism for throwing up alternative styles and policies of government.

VALHALLA

On the wealthy Chicago North Shore, Valhalla is the kind of community many Americans are aiming for and others dream of when they think of lucky gambles and "getting the breaks." An older, but not an old suburb, it is almost completely built up; its tree lined streets and spacious lawns make clear its rank as one of the wealthiest communities in America. (One of its census tracts showed in 1950 an average education for adults of 15.9 years schooling.) There is little ambivalence about the collective image of Valhalla; it is largely achieved and appreciated by its residents.

With its building complete and its land absorbed, there is little question of Valhalla's future. It is decided. Furthermore, its wealth allows a highly evaluated school system and an efficient and honest governmental administration. Its technical head is a well paid city manager, and its political process is carried on through a single party system: the Good Government Party is the only party in Valhalla. A group of several hundred people selected by invitation, the Party writes the platform for each new council and selects the slates of nominees for office. They win the ensuing election.

The political style of Valhalla is conditioned by the wealth and eminence of its citizens. Nobody seeks office in this community; the office (through the agency of the Good Government Party) seeks the man. It is a form of government from which politics, the struggle to determine the collective destiny, has been almost completely abolished. There is such consensus on communal destiny that no issues can arise. Consequently, the council is basically a watchdog organization which occasionally makes key decisions on questions of public finance; the machinery of government is in the civic bureaucracies controlled by the appointed city manager. He is the local expert, but his expertise does not awe a council made up of corporate executives, attorneys, and highly successful businessmen. Instead, they choose to trust him with the tedious details. It is a highly personalized government, a friends and neighbors atmosphere in which strong political opposition would be construed as a social insult, or a violation of the norms of good citizenship and neighborliness. Conflict is assiduously avoided, and most major decisions of the Council are unanimous.

In general, the population is not terribly concerned one way or the other with its governmental process. Although a minority, at most, can name any given official (the city manager is most widely known) and a very small minority ordinarily votes, the majority is usually overwhelmingly satisfied with their governance. Though they do not know the details of their government, they assume they could find out if they needed to; they are certain that any complaints will be attended in City Hall. (Thus general education does not translate directly into political competence: instead, it seems to produce a high degree of *self-confidence* with respect to the governing system.)

Issues are rare in such a political order. Usually the council devotes a great deal of time to trivia, the slight questions of equity which are a little out of the ordinary and cannot be easily settled by the hired administrator. Changes in zoning, waivers of regulations, and the like, constitute the order of business. Of course major financing is sometimes required; under these circumstances the collective financial wisdom of the council is usually regarded as an adequate substitute for the democratic process. Though citizens may be heard in open hearings, the decision is after all up to the council.

Such a system is poorly suited to handle basic conflict. In recent years one such issue did arise and it divided the community in half. The council decided to sell the municipally owned utilities, a heritage from the days when private enterprise would not gamble on the profitability of investment in Valhalla. The issue was hardly one of socialism versus capitalism (though one wit suggested it all started when the councilmen got fed up with being teased as "municipal socialists" down at the Union League); instead, it was a question of fidelity to the existing system, for the councilmen had run on the Good Gevernment Party platform, pledging continued municipal ownership of the utilities.

The news of the council's plans became current a few days before the municipal elections. In five days' time, a write-in slate was organized and a campaign mounted. In the resulting election, which drew an unprecedented half of the registered voters, the difference between the two slates was less than two percentage points. So close was the election that the losers filed for a recount; this was withdrawn when the council authorized a referendum on the utility sale. Again, the turnout was spectacularly high, and the sale was defeated by nearly two to one.

This battle was popularly considered to have created a long-lasting schism in the body politic. However, in a study of the community carried out two years later, the schism was found to be largely myth. The residents of Valhalla remembered it, to be sure; the astonishing proportion of 85 per cent volunteered it in answer to an open-ended question about "public issues in the past few years." But the vast majority considered it settled, and settled to its satisfaction. Furthermore, the citizens as a whole were perfectly satisfied with their governmental system; they felt well represented and bore no grudge. Thus the political order of Valhalla would appear, by the sternest test, to be a remarkably stable one. After extreme conflict, it had returned to its previous state of balance. The polity apparently rests upon a widespread comity, the political system upon a well-knit social system.

Reports upon these two suburbs cannot, of course, be generalized. There is a wide variation in suburbia. But we can note the difference brought about by rapid change, and the relative stability and placidity of the suburb whose basic destiny is clear. A word is in order about two other variations in the underlying population, however, social rank and urbanism.

We have been discussing two high-rank social aggregates. They are appreciably above the average for any metropolitan area. With lower social rank, with less economic surplus at the household level and therefore less at the governmental level, we expect the problems of the polity to change. We expect, for example, greater concern for the level of taxes and for the cost-benefit relationship. Public finance becomes a major issue, as Wood demonstrates in his large-scale study of metropolitan New York. In some working-class suburbs one finds a one-party system of the "tax-panicked," led by demagogic small-business men who are also painfully sensitive to the property tax.

In areas of lower social rank one also finds a growing discrepancy between the prestige and rewards of office and the position of the ordinary citizen. In Valhalla, nobody in elected office would think of accepting a salary; in a St. Louis County town of blue-collar and clerical workers, the $50.00 a month paid a village official may mean a second car for the family, or a new patio. The same is true of the other rewards of office, prestige and power. Men who are presidents of international corporations accept public office as a duty in Valhalla; it is a local recognition of accomplishment elsewhere. In working-class suburbia, the achievement of public office is itself a claim to fame. Consequently, as the social rank of the population goes down there is less likelihood of the office seeking the man. The differential value of political rewards is a key to variations in the political process of municipal government.

We have noted the increasingly urban life-style of the older suburbs, particularly those nearest the central city boundary. Evanston, Illinois, just outside Chicago, is one such city; University City in St. Louis County is another. Such cities, with many of the physical attributes of the central city and with increasingly old structures, tend to develop a permanent concern for the violation of housing codes, the deterioration of neighborhoods, and the possibilities of redevelopment. As they are forced to provide more of the typically urban services, as police forces and welfare agencies expand, they also become interested in raising the property tax base through industrial development and the like. They become, in short, little incorporated fragments of the central city. And as their population becomes more ethnic and urban, and eventually lower in social rank, they are increasingly likely to develop a partisan politics. Democratic and Republican clubs begin to figure in local elections. Issues arise with change in the underlying population, for such change causes a radical reappraisal of the inherited images of the community.

In summary, suburban political issues result from the questions posed to the community. These questions are derived from the immediate locale, and their chief relevance is usually seen as strictly local. The suburban development is in most respects simply a continuation of the rapid expansion of the urban plant which began in the middle of the nineteenth century. Bands of home-seekers settled the hinterland, in the housing created by large-scale development firms. Commerce and eventually industry followed, developing a texture of sites for human activity rather different from that in the older central city, but of a piece with the continuous results of increasing scale. The separate incorporation of these suburban enclaves in thousands of small municipalities rested upon the old democratic dogma "the right to local self rule."

The results are, however, startling in the aggregate. The development of order within each tiny community has no necessary effect upon the development of order between communities, or throughout the metropolitan area. In fact, order within the sub-community contributes to a sum of disorder, conflict, and inability to act for the metropolis as a whole. These phenomena will now be examined in detail.

Suggested Readings

Suburbia: Its People and Their Politics, Robert C. Wood, Boston: Houghton Mifflin, 1959. This is a provocative discussion of the origins of suburban settlement and incorporation, the nature of suburban political issues, and the type of government developed. The ideology of the "republic in miniature" is a source of fascination to the author, as it seems to both obscure and explain suburban political fragmentation.

The Suburban Community, W. A. Dobriner, editor, New York: G. P. Putnam's Sons, 1958. This volume includes empirical studies and theoretical essays dealing with the demographic, political, economic, and other aspects of the suburban population. While it lacks any integrated point of view, one may learn something about suburbia from several points of view.

"The Social Structure and Political Process of Suburbia," Scott Greer, *American Sociological Review,* 24: 514–526. This is an effort to develop a systematic theory of the community of limited liability in the suburbs. Neighborhood and local residential community are related to the polity of the suburban municipality, and the participational types discussed in this chapter are derived from this argument.

"The Suburban Dislocation," David Riesman, in "Metropolis in Ferment," *The Annals of the American Academy of Political and Social Science,* 314 (November, 1957). A thoughtful discussion of the effects suburbanization is likely to have upon participation, socialization, and the culture of America. On the whole, Riesman takes a gloomy view.

Part III

The Future of the Metropolity

6

The Schizoid Polity
and the Drive for
Reunification

The governmental dichotomy of the metropolis and fragmentation of suburbia have serious consequences for the total urban complex. First of all, the political processes are in no sense those of a unified metropolitan community. They are limited by the forces in play in each of the various subparts of the area, though the consequences of these forces may be very general. Furthermore, this fragmented polity confronts problems that are areawide in their origins, affecting all parts of the metropolitan area; they are problems which seem, logically and technically, to demand an areawide governmental response. Such a response, however, is difficult to imagine in an urban complex made up of a hundred or a thousand separate govern-

mental jurisdictions. Let us look at this aspect of the
metropolitan governmental structure in some detail.

Consequences of the Dichotomy: I. The Political Process

We have already noted the most dramatic consequence
of the dichotomy for urban politics: the separation of
numbers and wealth. Those who live in the green neighborhoods of suburbia have saved their families and homes
from the central city, at the price of valuable hostages left
behind. Their property (if they are wealthy) is most likely
to be located in the old center; banks and department
stores, utilities and factories and transport facilities, have
immense investments in the central city. The taxes they
pay, the governmental services they receive, their regulation
and protection by government, are all decided in a political
order of which they are not even citizens. Even if suburbanites are salaried managers and professionals, or wage
workers, they still depend on the city for a workplace; but
from the point of view of the central-city resident the
suburbanites have abandoned the central city. They pay
their property taxes on homes in Valhalla, Elm Village,
Meadowlane. Meanwhile, they return to the city each day
in droves, using the streets and sidewalks, claiming police
and fire protection—demanding and getting a fair share of
the central city's public services without paying the tax bill
that the residents of the city must shoulder.

Thus the power of city government is in the hands of
the central-city electorate, while great investments affected
by government are owned, managed, and manned by suburbanites. What wonder that many suburban residents are
concerned with central city government? Their concern
stems also from another kind of investment—the pious
dependence of suburbia upon the old central city as a clearinghouse, a symbol, a permanent center for the scattered
metropolitan region. Though he only returns occasionally

after work for the night life and the cultural events, the Loop, Manhattan, and the City of San Francisco still represent to the metropolitan citizen the social unity of the metropolis. If he sees it declining in looks, wealth, and activity, he is disturbed. Yet he is no citizen there; he has neither power nor responsibility for the center; he is a commuter.

As we have seen already, the governmental boundary lines between center and peripheries divide populations which differ on other counts. The variations result in a skewed distribution of both the central city and suburban electorates. Those who seek office in the center must appeal to the ethnics, the nonwhites and the foreign-born, the Catholics and Jews. They must also appeal to the working class, the blue-collar manual laborers, those who ordinarily vote the Democratic Party's ticket. Thus the ethnic organizations, the National Association for the Advancement of Colored People, and the B'nai B'rith, are important in central-city politics, along with the Catholic Church, the A.F.L.-C.I.O. Central Labor Council, and the Democratic Party's ward and precinct officials. Appeal to such organizations and the interests they represent is quite different from an approach to the total range of urban voters. Somebody is missing.

The missing persons are, of course, the middle-class native white Protestants who moved to suburbia. Though they are still weighty factors in the outer wards of the city (they can, for example, change a Democratic mayor's winning percentage from 60 to 75) they are preponderantly in the suburbs and continue to move outwards. These folks were once the electoral base of the Republican Party in the city; they also provided the cadres for the party's organization, the men who were willing to invest time and energy and money in the party's fortunes. They are now involved in the country's politics, or those of their diminutive suburbs. Nobody takes their place in central-city politics.

The progressive withdrawal of the upper occupational, educational, and income levels from the central city has produced a governmental segregation by social class. Each of the two great divisions in American society, the middle class and the working class, has its own government in the metropolis, and the existence of these structures means that they are used for class interests. At the same time, the separation of the two prevents the development of a governmental process which would act as a clearinghouse, adjudicating the claims of different interests within the society, producing definitive decisions on conflicting and uncertain positions. The dichotomy makes it extremely difficult for any group of men to act for the area as a whole. The mutual suspicion between central city and suburb becomes a political platform for aspirants to office in each part of the metropolis, just as that between "downstate" and the "city" provides political fuel for campaigns at the state level. Even informal cooperation suffers in the process.

Yet the metropolitan area is in many respects an interdependent whole. Suburbia could not exist for a week without the continual transfer of value from the workplaces of the central city to the suburban households. The opposite is also true: key posts in the economic organization of the central city are manned by those who live in suburban villas. And the whole will continue to experience rapid and widespread change and major challenges. (The fantastic prediction of fifty million new residents in the next two decades, most of them suburban, the lion's share of them in urban complexes already large and old, guarantees a continuous series of challenges to the social and governmental order.) But it is difficult to see any concerted response from the scramble of governments we have described. Each will pursue its own interests and problems within its existing framework.

Consequences of the Dichotomy: II. The Governmental Process

A useful way to approach the governmental process is to ask: What kinds of problems is it supposed to solve for the governed? We shall examine three types: (1) those resulting from the inescapable housekeeping problems of the city, (2) those produced in deciding the distribution of costs and benefits (or problems of equity) and (3) those deriving from the development of long-term control aimed at deciding the future shape of the metropolis. Each is radically affected by the dichotomy between central city and suburbs.

Most of the housekeeping problems of our metropolitan areas today are as old as cities. Julius Caesar struggled with the problems of transport in a growing Rome; city streets hardly wide enough for two carts to pass were forced to handle the flow of people and goods for a population rapidly approaching a million. Tenement dwellings were forever collapsing or catching fire because building contractors cheated, and because obsolete heating equipment was used in the housing of the poor. The streets at night were controlled by gangs of thieves and kidnappers, while sugar was sanded and milk was watered. The householders were apt to deposit their refuse in public places for others to walk through and carry away for them, while the supply of water was a perennial problem (leading to the construction of aqueducts which still stand and function in some places). In short, the urban problems of circulation, of energy input and waste disposal, and of public health and order emerged in Rome, as in Pittsburgh, and continue to appear wherever many live together in the interdependence of contiguity and exchange.

The tasks are clear. Political decisions arise with respect to such questions as these: How much service shall be provided, and how shall it be distributed among the citizens? The preconditions for answering these questions are (1) adequate technologies and (2) adequate resources of money and power. Our society of large and increasing scale has been fortunate in developing physical technologies; our potential power to control our environment is far greater than that of any previous society. However, the sheer volume and the rate of growth are also greater than they

have been before. As for the resources needed to carry on
the tasks we are, in some ways, poorer. In short, many of
our metropolitan housekeeping problems exist because we
do not pay enough to do a good job. In some degree, this
results from dividing our public treasury (our "fisc") into
too many bits and pieces, but in a large degree it results
from parsimony. Our inadequate governmental powers,
on the other hand, are more largely due to fractionated
jurisdictions (though the Jacksonian dogma has kept a close
curb on all expansions of governmental power). The political process does not allocate enough money and power
to provide the kinds of services many urbanites expect
from government.

THE PROBLEMS OF PROVIDING SERVICES

The provision of an efficient transportation grid for the
metropolis requires a tremendous material investment. It
also requires a unification of control patterns, so that traffic ordinances and police forces do not change every mile
or two. It requires an areawide power, for the components
of the problem situation are areawide in origin and effects.
Traffic generated in the suburbs flows to the central city,
while the central city's labor force pours back towards the
suburbs in the evening. For instance, a change in the
traffic ordinances of a suburban country town meant to
improve the main street as a shopping street for that community, may result in serious snarls on the freeways of the
central city. And the central city's express highway, ending
on a suburban road, may suddenly funnel two or three
times as much traffic through the village as had been expected by the village government. All efforts at control of
circulation in the metropolis must include suburbs and
central city, for the former usually provide the majority
of the automobiles in movement. Such efforts, to be effective, must also take into account other aspects of trans-

portation; terminals, public transport, parking arrangements and the like. Only broad areawide power can be
effective.

The same holds true for water supply and waste disposal.
Because water tends to organize its flow in a given depression (called a drainage basin), and because such a depression usually includes more than one governmental unit,
the actions of one suburb affect another, and suburbs affect
the drainage system of the central city. The St. Louis
County municipality that empties its sewage into an open
creek that runs through a neighboring town is, like the
Roman burgher emptying his slops in the public square,
an indication that the control system does not "fit" the
interdependent populations. However, in the St. Louis
County case, the "bad actor" was a government, standing
for an entire municipal population. Solutions to such
bad actions must obviously affect governments in their
responses to housekeeping problems. The metropolitan
household is in many respects one; but its housekeeping is
organized in dozens or hundreds of families, each indiffer-
ent to (if not hostile to) the neighbors.

Thus the central city is perennially in need of close
coordination of its services with those of the suburbs.
Lying towards the waterways and the railroads (a heritage
of its past in the Age of Steam), it is the ultimate recipient
of many flowing waters. Including as it does the major
part of the workplaces for the area, it is also the recipient
of the densest traffic. Fanned out in the suburban fringes,
traffic comes to a dense focus at the center of the arterials.
Here, in the central city, the worst aspects of urban automobile traffic are continually on view. The central city
resident, for whom the center is a "convenience shopping"
area, must drive through the concentrated traffic of the
entire metropolis in order to do his weekly shopping.

The suburbs also run into augmented problems as a
result of their fragmentation. They suffer the consequences
of spatial contiguity and resulting interdependence. Stu-

dents of metropolitan government are fond of remarking that polluted air and water, crime and fire and hydrogen bombs, are no respecters of our divided jurisdictions. Indeed, fragmentation may increase our vulnerability; the juvenile gang which takes care never to be booked in the home community cannot be identified if no central records exist. It may with impunity commit depradations in other suburbs and return home safely. As for such growing governmental tasks as preventive public medicine or disaster control (a standby organization to handle the results of flood, tornadoes, and nuclear war), the governmental patchwork makes them utterly impractical. The municipalities in most cases simply cannot afford professional services of these kinds. Their legal autonomy can, however, effectively prevent the areawide organization essential to the evacuation of populations or the rapid identification of health menaces. In short, the housekeeping problems of the individual governments, suburban as well as central city, are greatly increased by the political fragmentation of metropolitan areas.

THE PROBLEM OF EQUITY

A second kind of problem situation common in our metropolitan areas is that of equity. Because we have no areawide government, we have no areawide polity. As we have noted, this means that Negroes and other ethnics, union members, and wage workers tend to be represented most heavily in the central city; white-collar workers are concentrated in suburbia, where they are represented by a plethora of tiny governments. But the problem arises when a given area must pay for services to another—when the taxing jurisdiction does not include those who benefit from the taxes. In such cases, the result is literally taxation without representation.

We have noted the central city's position, as workplace

for the area and as central point of assembly. Important as its tasks are for the entire metropolis, it is not reimbursed by the villages of the fringe. It houses the poor, the unskilled and semiskilled laborers essential to many industries whose management lives in suburbia. These central-city populations produce far more than their share of the welfare and police problems of the area, just as they pay less than their share of taxes. They are net losses to the central-city government. At the same time the central city houses more of the areawide facilities of the metropolis—parks and museums and zoological gardens, convention halls and concert halls and theatres, universities and hospitals and trade schools. This land is ordinarily removed from the tax rolls; services must be provided for such sites, yet they cannot be taxed because they are nonprofit public enterprises. A similar loss results from the increasing network of superhighways which center in the older city; such roadways usually are built at the cost of millions of dollars in taxable property. They make the center accessible to suburban residents and the city pays. In short, the cost of services stays the same or increases in the central city, while the sources of revenue are declining. The question arises: What is fair in this kind of situation? Who should pay, and how much should they pay? There is no polity which includes all interested parties: those who own property pay, those who choose to do so drive in and use the facilities.

All is not clear sailing in suburbia, either. In Robert Wood's felicitous phrase, the suburban fragmentation results in "the segregation of resources from needs." The industrial plant which provides jobs for thousands of suburban workers pays taxes only to the little village in which it stands. Its work force, however, may double the school enrollment in another municipality to which the plant pays nothing. The suburban governmental wall provides immunity to taxation which might represent the total social cost of private enterprise, just as it provides immunity to teen-age gangs. To be sure, the larger the municipality the less likelihood there is of such obvious segregation. As Wood remarks:

> The larger a municipality . . . the more chance it may have to encompass a balanced blend of expenditure-inducing factors. . . . Hence the less vulnerable it becomes to decisions made in the private sector (i.e., the economy).[1]

However, as we have noted, most suburbs are not very large in either population or statute miles. Under such conditions, "historical caprice, in the form of ancient boundary lines, disrupts the pattern of regularity . . . the location of a single industrial plant, the decision of a developer . . . insignificant elements in the total urban complex of the region—drastically affect the public fortunes of the jurisdiction."[2]

Such eccentricity in the location of boundaries and the composition of suburbs results in statistics which many find disturbing. In St. Louis County one school district has an assessed valuation (the basis for all property taxes) which is *twenty-eight times the tax base per capita of another*. The first suburb pays one of the lowest tax rates in the area, the second, one of the highest. But the school systems are far apart in quality. The first is a superior school system, the second is struggling to maintain its accreditation. In fact, suburban municipalities vary so greatly in the amount and quality of services provided that many protagonists of metropolitan government base their arguments on the need for enforcing a mimimum standard of services in the suburbs. While some municipalities are as rich as Valhalla, many others are already paying higher taxes than the central city and providing poorer services. They can look forward to nothing but an astronomical increase in costs as the child population grows, settlement grows dens-

[1] Robert Wood, *1400 Governments, The Political Economy of the New York Metropolitan Region* (with the assistance of Vladimir V. Almendinger) Cambridge: Harvard University Press, 1961, p. 62.
[2] *Ibid.*, pp. 60–62.

er, and the school system, the street system, and police and fire protection become more expensive. For such suburbs, the question of equitable taxation is a pressing one indeed. But within the existing governmental framework they have no local resources beyond the taxes they can levy upon themselves.

The creation of an acceptable equity is, of course, a universal problem of government. It is usually solved through the adjudication of the political process which, within a framework of precedent (that is, a constitution), allocates costs and benefits in view of probable political repercussions. The peculiar nature of the problem in the metropolitan complex results from the governmental segregation caused by fixed boundary walls. The levying of taxes and use of social capital for social purposes can apply only to that segregated part of the population within the boundaries. The governmental redistribution of wealth which takes place wherever citizens pay unequal taxes and receive equal benefits (or vice versa) is also constrained by the boundaries. Instead of resulting from the political process it is ground out by the unequal units brought into being as the entrepreneurs incorporate municipalities on the fringe.

THE PROBLEM OF CONSENSUS: WHAT KIND OF CITY?

These effects of governmental fragmentation on the polity are clear. But in addition to the housekeeping problems and the moral problems of paying for them, we should also remember that the entire destiny of the metropolitan community is affected by its governance. Many aspects of the city which are today considered problems result from uncontrolled and unplanned development in the past. The tremendous investment of the past remains, as the layout of the community. Thus the question arises: Are contemporary developments any less likely to create future problems? Is the development in one part of the area considered in its relation to another? Are both viewed as generators of the future city? Is that city one that we wish to create?

Those who raise such questions are sometimes social idealists, Utopians who can imagine a city different from and better than the historical facts among which we live. Some are oriented to the past; for them the true nature of the city lies in the highly centralized urban complex whose people all live within one polity and one community. Looking backwards to the days when the city was a whole, they aspire to a new version in the future. Other Utopians are committed to a version of the city as even more dispersed, one in which the density and indignity of crowded streets and sidewalks would give way to dispersed concentrations of workplaces, residences, shopping malls, and community centers, surrounded and separated from others by miles of green countrysides.

Perhaps there is a little of this idealism in the thought of anyone concerned with the future of his city. Many persons also worry about future developments because action is demanded *at this very moment*. Without knowing what will happen in other parts of the metropolis and in the following years it is not possible for them to make very dependable plans, yet they *must* try to plan. The massive program of urban redevelopment, which aims at rebuilding large segments of the central city, requires that its managers be able to guess what will happen in other parts of the metropolis: the suburban neighborhoods, the giant shopping centers in the outer wards, the industrial satellite cities. They need to know what the market will be for their redeveloped sites. Equally important, those who are pushing to the forefront of urban settlement in the suburbs need to know what is going to occur in the center. Both urban redevelopers and suburban housing developers need to know where the important sites of work will be tomorrow, where the commercial centers will be, and how the transportation network will develop.

Such problems become extremely specific and tangible to the decision makers. They know, for example, that the planning of a new thoroughfare to relieve traffic congestion is not an isolated act. The new thoroughfare will open new neighborhoods to settlement (it will change the space-time ratio from workplace to residence) ; the new neighborhoods will provide for new populations which will use the thoroughfare (and probably crowd it) ; they will also require streets, sidewalks, parks, playgrounds, sewerage systems, and (most expensive) school systems. Thus the building of an expressway is more than a means of solving a traffic problem; after it is in being, it affects the very structure of the city, and its consequences become the basis for the future actions of the planner. Similar examples could be given for the interdependence of other aspects of urban development. Inescapable interdependence is not limited to the population of one governmental unit; as we have shown in detail, growth and development cut across the mosaic of governments.

It is not possible to plan development in the present metropolis. The simple collecting of information is a difficult if not impossible task for the hundreds of governmental units. The exercise of control "across the board" is absolutely impossible. Thus neither the Utopians nor the practical planner have much basis for predicting the effects of their actions: but if they cannot do this, they cannot plan at all. The metropolis continues to grow as in the past at a rapid rate, and like Topsy, it "jest grows." The effects of today's expansion of the urban plant will be tomorrow's metropolitan problems.

The Drive for Reintegration

Many observers have noted the consequences of governmental fragmentation in the metropolis. Whether they are government officials facing serious problems in rising costs and declining revenues, party leaders who see their cohorts reduced to impotence, technicians who despair of achieving their missions, political scientists, or simply metropolitan citizens, they come to similar conclusions. The obvious solution is based upon the cause: the small-scale governments of suburbia. Most observers conclude that these must be integrated in a larger structure and the governmental dichotomy reduced to unity. In short, they prescribe a metropolitan area government.

There are three kinds of formulas typically invoked. First, there are those who imagine an urban county, with most of the municipal powers exercised through the encompassing structure of the county while cities as such disappear. Second, there are those who wish to keep as many municipal structures in existence as seems practical. They advise a metropolitan district government for the solution of metropolitan problems, a large-scale structure encompassing the area but leaving many tasks to the smaller units of suburbia and to the central city's existing government. Finally, there are those who take their stand in the city and fight for "irredentism," the return of the lost territories of suburbia to their rightful polity, the central city.

In general, it appears that those who prescribe an urban county focus their vision on the suburbs. The symbol of the county is an all-encompassing one, bypassing the schism between central city and suburbs. Those who recommend a metropolitan district are "realists" who try to allow for the suburban society already in being and incorporated, while integrating the governmental response to the inescapable tasks of the area as a whole. Those who fight for merger are, in general, patriots of the central city. For them there is no metropolis except that which rightfully centers in downtown St. Louis, Cleveland, San Francisco, or Miami.

Technical evaluation of these three alternatives is fairly consistent, from observer to observer and state to state.

Within the provisions of most state constitutions the county is a very limited administrative arm; thus to create an urban county government is essentially to invent a new form of local government, and, having invented it, to insert it in the constitution. This is a complex and politically difficult task. The metropolitan "federal district" runs into similar difficulties; the division of tasks between areawide government and the municipalities is a mare's nest of legal conundrums. How can traffic be divided between areawide and local streets? They are interdependent. How can zoning become areawide in its efficiency while leaving the power to protect the neighborhoods to the municipality? And so on. Such problems are not insoluble; they are merely complex and, again, politically difficult. The outright merger of all the urban area in one big city usually runs into only one purely technical difficulty—the spread of metropolitan complexes across county, state, and in some instances (such as El Paso-Juarez and Detroit-Windsor) national boundary lines. Could we merge all urban population in one municipality, however, it would then be relatively simple to adapt the existing legal rights of cities to the tasks created by the total metropolis.

THE HISTORY OF METROPOLITAN GOVERNMENT PLANS

These are the most general recommendations of political scientists and other experts on metropolitan government. They are by no means new ideas. Writing in 1933, R. D. McKenzie noted the rapid growth of metropolitan areas and the increasing spread of population across existing political boundaries. He thought that "The larger cities of the country are becoming what might be termed regionally conscious."[3] He observed that even then efforts to

[3] "The Rise of Metropolitan Communities," in *Recent Social Trends, in The United States,* New York: McGraw-Hill Book Company, 1933, p. 451.

reintegrate suburbs and central city in one government had been made in Pittsburgh, St. Louis, and Cleveland; he thought that, despite the failure of these attempts, they would be made again. He was right. The Governmental Affairs Foundation recently published a digest which summarized nearly a hundred surveys of metropolitan areas made in the past twenty years. And efforts have been made again and again in such cities as St. Louis, Cleveland and Pittsburgh.

The results have been failure, in city after city, time after time. This failure reflects the existing dichotomy of the metropolis and the resulting political schizophrenia. In 1959, St. Louis held a referendum on a Metropolitan District Plan. It was a scheme developed by a Board of Freeholders and based largely upon the recommendations of the Metropolitan St. Louis Survey (a large-scale study of local government by social scientists) ; it was sponsored by many of the civic leaders of the community. It was well publicized by campaigns in the daily newspapers and was not vociferously opposed by the existing structures of government. Nevertheless, it lost by two to one in the central city, by three to one in the suburban county. The compromise solution had very little appeal.

There has, however, been one successful campaign for a metropolitan government. Perhaps we can learn something about resistance to such a government through looking at the campaign which, in 1957, resulted in a metropolitan Dade County government.

Dade County, the Greater Miami Metropolitan Area of Florida, is a new metropolis. At the time of the campaign for "Metro," half of the population had lived in the area for less than ten years. A medium-sized city, it had been flooded by migrants since World War II. As a result, the governmental machinery was overburdened, the revenues were inadequate to service the hundreds of thousands of new migrants, and such crucial services as sewerage disposal were nonexistent in many parts of the area. The political order was also rocked to its foundations; hundreds of new neighborhoods, dozens of communities, rose in a year or two without becoming integrated in the existing system. (The one-party regime also encouraged such looseness, for party discipline is still practically unknown in Dade County politics.) Under these circumstances there was little commitment to existing governments; the City of Miami came within eight hundred votes of being abolished as recently as the 1950's. Nor was there much loyalty to a discredited political order. The campaign for Metro was thus supported by all of the civic leaders and symbols of governmental virtue, while the opposition was practically silent. Yet, under such circumstances, the Metro plan won by only a few hundred votes.[4]

The campaign for Metro was, however, a costly one. In devising "a package that would sell" to the voters, the government that emerged was very weak. The Plan provided for little new revenue, though its backers promised that it would create all the governmental facilities needed in Dade County. It also failed to provide for any responsible governmental head: the Metro District was to be run by a County Manager, who served at the pleasure of an elected Council. The powers of the County were divided again and again with the existing municipalities; this created a potent source of centrifugal tendencies as each neighborhood or community jealously fought for its identity and privileges, making its voice heard through its elected representative. Then too, in the campaign for Metro one of the major selling points of its protagonists was economy: the Metro government was expected to do many more tasks than had ever been performed before, at a net saving in taxes. Needless to say, the price for getting the approval of citizens in referendum elections is now being paid by the Metro government. It appears that it may have been too great a price to result in amelioration

---

[4] For a brief discussion of the campaign for Metro see Edward Sofen, "Problems of Metropolitan Leadership: The Miami Experience," *Midwest Journal of Political Science,* Vol. V, No. 1, pp. 18–38.

of the various metropolitan problems the plan set out to solve.

THE BARRIERS TO CHANGE

The difficulties of changing metropolitan governmental structure may be usefully divided into three levels. These are (1) the underlying cultural norms of Americans concerning local government, (2) the resulting legal-constitutional structures, and (3) the political-governmental system built upon them. The underlying norms are those described earlier as the Jacksonian ideology, the dogma of the right to local self-government and the direct exposure of the governmental system to the veto of the voters. Shared by citizen and political leader alike, these norms are important because they specify *what is legitimate*. Based upon a deep distrust of governmental officials and a faith in the competence of the ordinary voter, they also lead to such corollaries as "that government is best which governs least" (and more important, *costs* least).

Translated into the legal provisions of the constitution, the norms set up the rules of the game. They validate the incorporation of municipalities for many purposes, including the trivial, spurious, and even socially injurious pursuit of self-interest. They also provide the mechanisms for changing the nature of local governments with the result that basic structural change must be submitted to the voters in referendum. In that referendum, the citizen does not act as an isolated, free-floating intelligence: he is, after all, an actor in an existing neighborhood, community, municipality. His political leaders are those who were elected through the present system, and are usually committed to it.

The existing political system is a major problem for any reform movement. Those who are committed to change are usually not the incumbents. Thus, reformers have to carry their message through the mass media and lectures, for they are disbarred from the political organizations. The "machine of the incumbents," however, can easily and quietly mobilize the existing system against change. Any change is a danger to the going concern, and those who benefit from existing arrangements see no gain in a radical departure. The public servant fears for his job; the contractor fears for his contract. Insofar as such persons are important reference points for voters, they encourage suspicion of anything new.

As for the ordinary voter, we can say something about his responses. In St. Louis a sample survey was taken immediately after the failure of the District Plan.[5] In general, it is clear that neither the protagonists nor the antagonists of reform "got through to the voter" very clearly. In the suburban sample, selected for past involvement in local elections, only 10 per cent of the voters had roughly correct notions of three most important provisions of the plan: its methods of governance, the effects on existing communities, and the tax rate authorized. Only about 20 per cent could state any of these major provisions correctly. Thus the ordinary voters were not even voting on the plan: nobody knows what they *were* voting on.

However, there is little evidence that the campaign against the plan was effective. The voters questioned afterward had never heard of most individuals for or against the plan (evidently civic leaders, the power elite, the economic dominants, talk chiefly to each other—and to social scientists studying the power structure). They were, if interested, more likely to know how the major mass media stood: still, only 49 per cent of them knew correctly the *Post-Dispatch's* position, after that dominant newspaper had put on an all-out three months' campaign for the plan.

The one major figure who seemed to have had an impact, and in the intended direction, was the mayor of the central city. Even in the suburbs a majority knew his posi-

[5] This research was carried out by the Center for Metropolitan Studies of Northwestern University. It will be reported in detail in the volume *Metropolitics, A study of Political Culture,* Scott Greer and Norton Long.

tion, respected it, and in many cases said it helped them to make up their minds. The dominant symbolic position of the central city mayor in metropolitan affairs is thus demonstrated again. However, most individuals and organizations involved in the campaign were unknown to the voters, and their position on the plan (if the voter ventured a guess) was as likely to be reversed as correctly stated. The political system simply does not function for this type of campaign, not at least as its functioning is envisaged in the democratic dogma.

The lack of interest, involvement, and information among the voters should not lead us to ignore what did occur in their political discourse. There are strong indications that the campaign, the talk back and forth, while it did not increase competence, did produce a high degree of confusion among the voters. Rhetorical tricks, the exercise of the journalist's skills, and a certain amount of sharp practice on both sides, left the voter some basis for guessing that: "The District Plan would tax us fifty cents on the dollar," or "The District Plan would abolish all governments and create one big city."

The confusion resulted, chiefly, in the evocation of the basic political norms controlling local government. Governmental merger and the loss of local control was a bad business. On the other hand, increased coordination and cooperation among the scattered local governments were good; with increased size go efficiency and economy. The improvement in governmental services was a fine thing. But an increase in taxes was a dreadful prospect, and the addition of "another layer of government" brought chills to some people's spine. In short, confusion led to the evocation of norms. These norms are frequently contradictory. The average citizen, hardly educated to the real nature of the plan, evoked rules of thumb as old as government: "Better the evil that is known . . ." and "When in doubt do nothing." These phrases summarize the final response of a great many among both leaders and led to the plan for a metropolitan government.

The campaign attempted, in a few months' time, to propagandize a complex scheme for applied social science. It was further handicapped by dependence upon the mass media. No wonder the *status quo* was victorious. The norms evoked, however, are not transitory matters: the basic conflict between the norms for local government and the rising consumption norms for governmental services seems to be a permanent part of our public discourse. Local governing bodies are trusted with neither the powers nor the material resources to provide increasingly expensive services: at the same time, they are blamed for their failure to provide them. Such a campaign as that for the District Plan dramatizes this conflict in the normative structure of the American political community. Its results also become part of that structure, for the campaign resulted in a certain amount of social learning.

Many citizens learned something from both sides in the conflict. They learned, certainly, that much better services in the area of traffic facilities and transport could be provided for the metropolis. They also learned that efficiency, coordination, cooperation, were good things (as long as they cost nobody any taxes or local autonomy). In short, they learned some of the campaign slogans. The leaders of the campaign also learned. Some concluded that the District Plan, a compromise between the interests of central city and suburbs, satisfied nobody; it lacked "box office appeal." They decided that only an all-out campaign for one big city was capable of stirring the imaginations of the voters. But others (and probably the majority) decided that nothing could be done to create a metropolitan government through referendum elections.

When such an acknowledgement of defeat is common, the effort to restructure the government at the most general level is abandoned, often for a decade or more. That which exists, the snarl of polities, the multiplying suburbs, the slowly changing central city, becomes the given nature of things. It is a "traditional system" by default: it is impossible to change. But what of the massive challenges which confront the metropolitan governments? How are they handled within the framework of a central city and hundreds of suburbs? We turn now to the existing polity, the bicycle with two warped wheels, which nevertheless manages to carry its rider without too many falls.

Suggested Readings

On The Schizoid Polity:

1400 Governments: The Political Economy of the New York Metropolitan Region, Robert C. Wood with the assistance of Vladimir V. Almendinger, Cambridge: Harvard University Press, 1961. Wood examines carefully the effects of the government on the private economy, and the return effects of economy on government. His general conclusions greatly deemphasize the effects of any likely governmental action on the over-all economy or social structure of the New York region.

Government and Housing in Metropolitan Areas, Edward C. Banfield and Morton Grodzins, New York: McGraw-Hill Book Company, 1958. In this study the authors attempt to decide exactly what effect the fragmented government of the metropolitan area has upon the housing distribution among the population, and what difference metropolitan governmental integration would make. Their general conclusions are that it would make relatively slight differences.

On The Drive for Reintegration:

"The Future Metropolis," *Daedelus,* Winter, 1961. This issue of the journal has a distinguished set of contributors whose general approach seems to reflect a growing conviction that the key elements in the development of the city are social and economic, with government and governmental planning relatively unimportant. The skepticism concerning the possibility of large-scale planning is a relatively recent development among such theorists.

7

The Metropolity and
Its Future

Galbraith has remarked that, according to the laws of aerodynamics, it is impossible for the bumblebee to fly. And according to the rules of some political theorists, it is impossible for anything resembling a metropolitan polity to function. Yet the bumblebee flies, and the metropolis meets, in some fashion, the consequences of massive change. The millions are housed, fed, transported, and policed, and the metropolitan region still maintains its attraction for the migrant. Smog and traffic and farcical contradictions in land use are commonplace in Los Angeles, yet it moves rapidly towards the status of second city in the nation. None of the urban ills in St. Louis prevents its continued growth and increasing prosperity.

SUBSTITUTES FOR METROPOLITAN GOVERNMENT

The metropolis is in little danger of a breakdown. The reason is partly that within the straitjacket of the democratic ideology and the constitutions, there is room to maneuver. Coordination takes place at the municipality level. There is a continuum, from voluntary consultation and joint planning among suburbs to those contractual arrangements which house the prisoners of many places in one suburb's jail or draw upon the county government for many basic services. Such consultation and cooperation is in fact the alternative to metropolitan merger proposed by the defenders of little governments. But voluntary co-operation requires an obvious interdependence, a nearly equal cost and benefit ratio, and a rational view of collective needs. It also depends upon an adequate public treasury. It suffers all the political weakness of confederations, and many major services are not possible through such arrangements. In these cases, two subterfuges have been widely adopted: the special district and outside subsidy.

The special district government emerged as an expedient solution for the problems of jurisdictional fragmentation. Created as a new governmental entity, the special district government has access to taxes and borrowing powers outside those granted the municipality. Bypassing the municipal government, it escapes both the jealous particularism of the elected council and the niggardliness of the citizens. Defined as outside the political process, it can apply the rules of thumb appropriate to a business enterprise. At the extreme, as in the case of the New York Port Authority, it can commandeer the most profitable tasks of government (toll bridges and tunnels and the like), pay its way, and have money to invest.

If we compiled a rough check list of the special district governments in the United States today, the total is staggering. School districts, water districts, fire districts, port districts, sanitation districts, park districts—the variety is almost as great as the tasks that local government can perform. Created on an *ad hoc* basis, as needs arise and the local fisc and powers prove inadequate, such districts are frequently the basis for the only adequate services in many suburbs. They are also, in many urban areas, the only metropolitan governmental unit in being. Such metropolitan giants as the New York Port Authority, the Metropolitan St. Louis Sewer District, the Chicago Park District, are partial solutions to some of the problems of metropolitan growth.[1]

However, there are narrow limits to their utility. The services that are their basis must be in wide demand: many needed services are not considered by the voters. Furthermore, only a few governmental services can be made profitable: most of them are "losers" and remain the prerogative of existing municipal governments. And the losers, whether organized in a special district or not, continue to demand a share of the limited fiscal powers of the jurisdiction. As the local resources (or those the voters will make available within the limits of the state's constitutional provisions) are exhausted in the existing functions of government, the pressure mounts for subsidy from elsewhere. The State government and the federal agencies are the chief sources of outside funds.

Through these channels come supports for the expenses of both central city and suburbs. The welfare burdens of the central city, such as aid to dependent children, aid to the handicapped, preventive medicine, clinics, hospitals, school lunches, and the like are greatly lightened by funds from elsewhere. The problems involved in rebuilding the obsolescent plant at the center of the city are turned over to the Urban Renewal Authority, a local recipient of massive federal grants. In the suburbs also the cost of plant expansion is lightened greatly by what Wood has called "the new Federalism." The Federal Highway Program, in building great new arterials and circumferential highways, solves many fiscal problems of the surburbs, and any aid

[1] Useful description and analysis of the New York area "metropolitan giants" is found in Sayre and Kaufman, and in Wood, *op. cit.*

to schools (especially that earmarked for buildings) will
be disproportionately distributed in suburbia, for the central city's educational plant is nearly complete. In suburbia,
too, welfare costs are passed upwards.

CONSEQUENCES OF USING SUBSTITUTES

These expedients have consequences for the situation
which brought them about. They are, for one thing, removed from the surveillance and control of the local voters,
and may be largely inaccessible to the politician and governmental official. Thus they violate the norm of local
self-rule and responsibility to the local voters. This is the
very reason for their creation: they bypass the local political process. Money and powers guarded jealously from
the central city and suburban municipalities are passed
upwards to Washington, from which they return free of
the political blame that local officials would have to bear.
Ironically, the net result of the system which keeps government "close to the people" is its removal as far as possible
from the people—to the United States Congress, a State
agency, or a Federal agency. Or, as with special districts,
the power is handed to agencies whose decisions are rarely
ever known to their clients, much less controlled by them,
agencies which have been dubbed "ghost governments."

Another important aspect of these expedients is their
segmental nature. Each task of government is handled without reference to others, even though their interaction is
crucial for the developing shape of the city and its welfare.
(It is not, at present, even possible to learn the total
resources and powers of the federal government engaged
in any given metropolis. Apparently *nobody* knows.) But
the increasing network of speedy trafficways continues,
blindly, the change in space-time ratio which produces the
suburban dispersion. As the arterials multiply, as the circumferential highways tie suburb to suburb, as the center

hub becomes a five-level interchange, the result can only be a continual stimulus to further centrifugal development. At the same time, however, the urban redevelopment program is investing billions of dollars in rebuilding the central city for its old uses—commercial, industrial, residential. Thus two massive programs are under way, each largely financed outside the metropolis, each the *raison d'être* for huge bureaucracies—and each directly contradicting the purposes of the other. The central city is declining as a useful site for activity precisely because of the land accessible in the suburbs; to renovate downtown sites while increasing the ease of movement outwards is to give with one hand and take away with the other.

In fact, the strongest argument for local determination of the crucial decisions in public capital expansion is based upon the effects of partial and unplanned action from above. Those who are neighbors, committed to the same metropolitan site and social system, *must live with the consequences of these decisions.* The shape of the city, the quality of services, the cost-benefit ratio, the nature of the public order, all of these aspects of urban government are peculiarly the burden of the population living in the area. Frequently there is no technical rule for a decision: when a freeway is located, some people will benefit at little cost, others will lose. Somebody's ox is always gored, and the democratic polity is in theory supposed to allow that person his day in court. This is not possible when autonomous agencies, local or federal, move without the consent of the governed.

To be sure, combining all functions and powers of government in the metropolitan area would not guarantee an integrated polity. There is ample evidence of lack of planning among the agencies of any central city government: the struggles of the great bureaucracies for survival and growth frequently resemble those of giant lizards in the jungles of the Jurassic Era. It is certain, however, that little coordination can come about in the present ecology of political orders: the power of legal autonomy is a strong shield against forced confrontation. Thus the planning agencies in a great city may live their lives in complete ignorance of each other; traffic engineers and urban renewal agency heads may be complete strangers. Nobody is accountable beyond the narrow limits of his designated task. The metropolitan polity is a net result: a continuous, cumulative total of the decisions made in suburban municipality, fire districts, metropolitan district, central city bureaucracy, county government, federal agency, and state bureau.

The Future Course of the Metropolis

The metropolis in being is, in many respects, a museum of the urban past. Because dense areas were built up for the City of Steam, because they represent social value derived from the funded energy of the past, we have today the near-obsolescence of much of the downtown. Because the suburbs developed outside the central city's jurisdiction we have today the patchwork quilt of jurisdictions on the outskirts. In short, we inherit our given conditions from the past, and they are largely unforeseen results of expediential decisions. It is fairly certain that the people of the metropolis are not concerned with governmental change that would allow more foresight in the future. What, then, can we expect to emerge from the present course of development?

Returning to basic considerations, we must remember that the process of increase in scale continues. History, the unfolding of consequences through time, does not stand still to be photographed. We may confidently predict a further increase in the societal surplus, a further decline in the time and money cost of movement, a further extension of the organizational networks. From these we certainly expect a continuing increase in the absolute and relative size of the United States' population living in metropolitan areas.

Increase in the societal surplus will result in a continuing upward movement in social rank for the entire population. Mechanization and the use of nonhuman energy sources will make unskilled labor obsolete; the increasing demand for rationality will increase the workforce in the areas of organizational control—those workers who manipulate symbols and persons. But mechanization will invade these areas also: electronic computers can store and process information much more rapidly and cheaply than their present day substitutes, the white-collar girls. Thus we will continue to experience a decline in routine jobs and an increase in those demanding specialized skills. The professional and semi-professional worker, the technician and the manager will increase at the expense of unskilled and semiskilled labor. To prepare for the former jobs, however, individuals will be forced to increase their formal education. Thus occupational and educational levels will go upwards together. The net effect of such a workforce, with its machines and sources of energy, will be a continuous increase in the social surplus: real income will rise concomitantly.

As this occurs, the range of social choice will also increase and will be available to more people. The choice between an urban and a familistic way of life will become a constant differentiator, as families at all levels of social rank have enough "elbow room" to choose how and, within limits, where they will live. With so many opportunities for advancement open, we may expect acculturation to progress further: most ethnic minorities should become largely invisible in a few decades. Thus the total population of the metropolis should approximate more and more closely the social class range of those now in suburbia.

The space-time ratio will continue to affect, drastically, the layout and population distribution of the metropolitan area. As highways reach further into the countryside, as the automobile-owning population becomes well-nigh universal, the spaces between arterials will fill in. Residential expansion on the fringes will accommodate millions of new urban residents in the immediate future. Urban redevelopment programs may try to attract them to the central city, but as Raymond Vernon has recently stated, "it is one of the paradoxes of urban growth today that the increase in the supply of urban land is probably outstripping the demand."[2] Automobile and roadway continually capture new domains for the metropolitan complex.

Changes in the space-time ratio for transport and communication will also allow continual decentralization of work. The further dispersion of work sites requires no decrease of effective centralized control, in the day of two-way telecommunication and jet travel. The sites for work and commerce will also move rapidly away from the center insofar as truck transport can take the place of rail and water. Leon Moses has recently documented the shift of truck terminals outwards in Chicago. They follow either the warehouses which follow the retail outlets, or the industrial plants which follow the most desirable labor force.[3] The economic map of the metropolis moves from a city with hinterland to a larger unit, in Vernon's terms a "region."

THE CHANGING TASKS OF THE CENTRAL CITY

Let us turn, then, to the consequences of these ongoing changes for the social structure of the metropolis. The central city's role, in a drama already different from one in which it played the lead and most of the characters, can be expected to alter further. As the nonsegregated and familistic populations move outward the city becomes in-

2 "The Economics and Finances of the Large Metropolis," *Daedelus*, Winter 1961, p. 46.
3 In a study carried out at the Transportation Center, Northwestern University, to be published in 1962.

creasingly the municipality of the ethnic and the working class. The remnants of the traditional urban working class, familistic, and usually first or second generation ethnic, will recede slowly from the neighborhoods that are their urban home. The colored populations will continue to increase at a steady rate. The continued upgrading of social rank will have a differential effect for these, most segregated and disprivileged segments of the society. Negroes, Puerto Ricans, and Mexicans, last in the urban labor force from the rural hinterlands, are concentrated in precisely the kinds of jobs most likely to be abolished by mechanization. They are also segregated within the wards of the central city. Thus the population of the center will shoulder a disproportionately heavy share of the social burdens produced by automation.

The center's residential function will be, then, more consistently biased towards the lower half of the job distribution. Its other functions can be expected to change slowly through time. As those activities that are more conveniently located in the suburbs depart, those that are best suited to the center will stand out in sharper relief. One obvious use for the center is the interchange, the crossroads for superhighways knitting the metropolitan map together. Another is that of exchange center for those items which require an areawide market. Still another use is that of a site for activities which require personal confrontation, those negotiations between firms and consultations with experts that must be conducted face to face. Nobody knows just how large these uses will bulk, in the aggregate.

Nor does anybody know how large the demand will be for the urbane living conditions of the center. We can expect those whose life-style fits the apartment-house districts to continue their residency; we do not know how large a proportion of the total they will be. We can also expect the wealthy to continue part-time residence in such places as Beacon Hill, Nob Hill, and Executive House. As many have pointed out, for the aged also a safe downtown apartment-house neighborhood may be preferable to the dispersed areas of suburbia. But factors of cost and budget, as well as the rarity of safe neighborhoods in many parts of the center, will probably limit the return of the "post-child" family to the urban center.

THE DEVELOPING SUBURBS

The suburbs should be, increasingly, a world inhabited by the lower-middle to upper social ranks of the metropolis. The raw, new neighborhoods will slowly settle in, with public facilities developed and horticulture softening the angles of the tract development. Though some persons have looked at the cheap neighborhoods built for craftsmen and operatives and predicted the slums of the future, this seems unlikely. Instead, the continuous input of time and energy and money by the suburban home owner, the do-it-yourself movement, can be expected to upgrade or at least stabilize these neighborhoods for many years. The decay of neighborhoods is a social phenomenon; as we have seen, suburban neighborhoods develop very powerful communication flows and a normative structure capable of educating the new neighbors. This in turn results in that regular input of energy which prevents age of structure from being synonymous with decay of structure.

Since the suburbs will include the richest markets for household consumables, the movement of convenience shopping outward will continue in full force. From neighborhood store to shopping center to the giant commercial subnucleus with its shopping malls, meeting rooms, and branches of downtown stores and banks, a regular system of retail dominance will develop. In large segments of the suburbs we can expect a partial reintegration of the lives of suburbanites; the giant subnucleus can produce a concentration of work places and contain the essential folk institutions of church, school, government, recreation, and the like. Since they will also contain a large proportion of friends and relatives, as well as the omnipresent neighbors, they may become self-contained social worlds for many of their inhabitants.

It is even possible that many activities now universally conceived of as best located in the downtown area may also move towards suburbia. The public arts, for example, music and theatre, ballet and the museums might well be decentralized. Their chief markets are, after all, the suburban populations. And with the development of convenient transport within the giant subnuclei, a touring company or a traveling exhibit could easily move from one area to another.

At the level of economic and social functions, the central city will continue to recede as the overwhelming force of the metropolis. Though for many it still maintains its magic as hub and symbolic center of the metropolitan community, it is in many respects simply one differentiated area of residence and work, equal among equals in the cluster of great subnuclei which make up the metropolis. Its proportionate size does not stand for a proportionate representation of the total urban population, and its polity is not that of the metropolitan region. Nor, given its biased sample of urbanites, could it be. Let us turn then to the probable developments of the polity in each half of the urban region.

The Future Polity

For each half of the metropolis we will ask: how does its nature condition the burdens of government, and what are its resources for handling those tasks?

The central city is the inheritor of the aged neighborhoods and the obsolete workplaces of a Paleotechnic city. Two movements are afoot to change this social heritage: the metropolitan government movement, and the urban redevelopment program. The first aims to solve the problem by reincorporating the center with all its sprawling suburbs into a new unity; we have already considered the problems and prospects of such an enterprise. The urban redevelopment program would appear almost equally hopeless, *if* one accepts the enthusiastic plans of some of its backers to remake the central city.

The central city of even a moderate-sized metropolis is an enormous plant. There are mile upon mile of neighborhoods built in another day, for other life-styles, and therefore depopulated by the kinds of people who once built them and lived in them. There are street after street of tall loft buildings, high rise elevator warehouses. These are now hopelessly obsolete in competition with suburban warehouses, whose horizontal floors allow the use of new and more efficient equipment (moving belts, fork lifts, and the like). There are hundreds of acres of neighborhoods whose street space, already far too narrow for contemporary vehicular traffic, must also provide parking, for the automobile was not envisaged when they were built. Though this plant has a social value (for the structures are often sound) it is not attractive to enterprises that are better situated in suburbia's new acres. It still has a market value, because it has uses: and those who wish to rebuild the city must confront these uses as reflected in market value. (The American norms of local government do not easily permit simple confiscation.) The price for purchase and demolition in most central cities has been estimated at $160,000,-000 and up per square mile: at the end of these processes one would have only a bare plot of ground. Such a site might or might not be valuable to private enterprise; to "write it down" to prices competitive with new land on the outskirts, however, would result in monstrous public costs.

Robert Wood has called the New York City Urban Renewal Program probably the most vigorously developed and certainly the largest in the United States. Yet if one includes work completed, in progress, or definitely planned for the future, only 1,000 acres will be affected.[4] His estimate is that 5,000 acres of New York City are already so far gone that they demand rebuilding—and by the time the work on the 1,000 is complete, there is every likelihood that the 5,000 total will remain approximately the same. Furthermore, Vernon has called attention to what he calls the grey areas, those far outside the central location (which he believes *does* have use value) and far gone in their obsolescence. For such areas he can foresee little demand, either as commercial or residential building sites. One might, in fact, wonder if urban redevelopment does not require eventually rebuilding the entire older city. Against such problems the present program, massive as it appears in isolation, is a drop in the bucket.

POLICY FOR THE CENTRAL CITY

The central city is not apt to change radically in its composition. Its people will be working class, ethnic, residents of neighborhoods ranging from the slums to the shabby genteel hand-me-downs of the past middle classes. If this is so, it will probably call forth specific kinds of governmental action. Instead of pouring public wealth into new building, hoping that a neighborhood will attract private investors, it will seem more relevant to spend money on the conservation of existing neighborhoods, working to protect existing homes through improvement, better public services, and most of all support of the existing communication and normative structures that lead to reinvestment in their maintenance.

If the central city is to be the workingman's municipality, its governors will eventually come to assess its programs with this fact in mind, rather than evoking its lost role of

4 See Wood, *op. cit.*

center and symbol to a region. Thus its educational needs will be defined as different from those of suburbia. Such institutions as the University of Pennsylvania, the University of Chicago, or the University of Southern California, private universities which service the suburbs and the nation, will be considered less relevant to the sons of workers and therefore to the city's polity than the "open door colleges." These publicly supported institutions must accommodate the increasingly large percentage of high school graduates who can and must go to college if they are to be useful members of the labor force. The educational system of the central city will also be forced to concern itself with the problem of retraining the technologically displaced, for the central city will inherit a large share of the social costs involved in such displacement.

The government of the central city can also be expected to accept the responsibility of housing, policing, educating, and servicing the neighborhoods of nonwhite minorities, rapidly becoming its single largest voting bloc. Segregation in housing and schools, and differential treatment by the agencies of government (particularly the police) is becoming politically inexpedient in the short run, foolhardy in the long run. While new land uses and new industry are important for the declining fiscal prowess of the city government, such new uses, as far as they further shorten the supply of housing available to nonwhites, are gift horses which will be subject to increasingly sharp inspection as nonwhites respond at the polls.

The resources available to the central city government in responding to its status and problems as a working-class municipality are changing rapidly. While the property tax base is slowly declining, a result of changing population and the increase in public facilities, new taxes are being invented. The earnings tax which applies to all who work in the city, suburbanite and city resident alike, amounts to a radical readjustment of equity. Departing from property as an index of use and ability to pay, the earnings tax is based upon the chief source of wealth in our society, income. The suburbanite, who uses the city for his livelihood, pays a share of the maintenance.

The suburbanite also pays as the federal government accepts more fiscal responsibility for the central city. The suburban personal income tax far outweighs that of the city. And we have already noted the present importance of federal funds for the metropolis. With the increasingly important role of urban affairs in the federal government, we can expect more subsidy, for renewal, conservation, education, and the like. Such funds can be used to adjust the present limits upon the life space of the nonwhite population: the conservation of neighborhoods and the broadened base for higher education would do much to level the present distinctions by color. As for the grey areas, as well as the miles of shabby genteel housing outside them, they may find their most suitable use as areas of open occupancy for those now crowded into the Negro ghettoes. The declining neighborhoods of the central city may be seen as a major resource for increasing the housing available to the segregated. Open occupancy combined with a sophisticated and well-financed program of neighborhood organizing, rebuilding, and conservation may solve several problems at once.

In short, if the central city is viewed in its new role as a specialized area in the metropolitan complex, a home for the working class and the ethnics, its situation is not so desperate. If it is viewed as still the major and most valuable part of the metropolis, one which should be inclusive of the total population, the symbol and hub of central tendencies in the entire urban complex, its future is dark. The arterials move outward month by month, the circumferentials circle the area in concentric rings, and the automobile becomes standard equipment. The fifty million new urbanites of the next few decades provide a long-run and lucrative market for continuous new development on the fringes. It is unlikely that the center can compete as the site for much of this new growth.

POLICY FOR SUBURBIA

In the suburbs the limiting conditions are also a result of past commitments. The dozens or hundreds of small jurisdictions also result from the governmental "freeze." Many of them have little or no space for industry, inadequate commercial districts, and no room for parks, playgrounds, and educational facilities, and they are landlocked by neighboring domains. Each enjoys a degree of autonomy, and the price is that of the isolated peasant village—it is alone with its fiscal and governmental problems. For the fortunate few in Valhalla, this is no problem; for many others it is a basic and continuing one.

The problems in the life-cycle of a suburb are as follows. First, the determination of land use, then the provisions of governmental facilities and resources, then the maintenance of the area's character, and finally the adjustment to change in the population. As the neighborhoods grow older they lose their competitive attraction for the social rank which built them, and are slowly invaded and eventually populated by a different class. Such change may be agonizing for the older inhabitants, committed financially and emotionally to their old image of the suburban country town with a pretty name. It will not be so agonizing, however, for most of those who might lead a fight to repulse the invaders, for they will already have moved on outward.

The resources available to the suburbs have been detailed. Massive and probably increasing federal aid for schools, roads, sanitation, and the like, augmented by such fiscal dodges as the special district, supplement the *ad hoc* cooperation among municipalities. To be sure, as the burdens of government press heavier on the fisc, there may be efforts to solve the problem by changing land use, attracting industry and other high tax-yield activities. However, such efforts are usually hamstrung by the very conditions which stimulate them; awareness of serious fiscal problems typically follows the building up of available sites. The time lag between public act and consequence (and the magic phrase "a city of homes") limits the political appeal of such efforts when they are still practical. But above all, the location of activities tends to result from position in the space-time grid of the city, not from the blandishments of local councilmen. As Wood says:

> With so many different constituencies, many options are open for firms and households alike, and though the process of industrial and population diffusion may occasionally be skewed, the forces are not, in general, thwarted, turned aside, or guided.[5]

As for the problems created by the slow change, the movement of a suburb downhill in the scale of housing values, there seems to be no real solution possible for any given unit. What occurs instead is the dispersion of the population to new areas now preferable to the old neighborhood. The continual increase in land resulting from the changing space-time ratio solves most of the problems of invasion by the same mechanism which brings them about in the first place, movement to new locales.

In summary, then, there is no polity which sees the metropolitan complex as a whole, continuous in time and interdependent in the present. The basic and pressing needs of the metropolitan population, as they can be translated into political pressure, result in new burdens for government. Thus the public sector of the economy, like the private sector, responds to those who can and will pay. The metropolitan citizen does not appear willing to pay in money or loss of local self-rule for a metropolitan government. He is willing to pay for special districts, area-

5 *Ibid.*, p. 112.

wide in scope, to solve his most pressing problems. Sewage disposal can be such a pressing problem. Traffic and transport may well become another interest which causes the electoral turnstiles to ring. If so, there will be metropolitan transportation systems under coordinated management. But transport, crucial as it is to many other public tasks and basic to the emerging shape of the city, will then function even more freely outside the pressures of other competing and legitimate interests. As Wood puts it:

> The highway transportation agencies, the mortgage programs of the Federal Housing Administration and Veterans Administration proceed on the same philosophy of supply and demand that governs the behavior of private firms. . . . The final result is that a public sector committed to this ideology by financing and structure offers no countervailing influence against the trends generated in the private sector. . . . They underwrite and accelerate the process of scatteration.[6]

This scatteration is more than physical. It is also a scatteration in social and political space, a separation of control and planning centers, and therefore a forswearing of the possibility of politically or technically rational policy. The conservative, steady state governments of the central cities drift towards a polyarchy of great bureaucracies largely moved and shaken by programs generated elsewhere. The patchwork governments of suburbia fight for their place in the sun of federal aid, hoping someone, somewhere else, will solve the problems of their collective destiny for them. Businessmen expect action from governmental officials: the politicians wait to bless any decision upon which interested parties can agree. As Morris Janowitz has put it: "The issue is not the manipulation of the citizenry by a small elite, but rather the inability of elites to create the conditions required for making decisions."[7]

6 *Ibid.,* p. 172.
7 "Introduction," to *Community Political Systems,* edited by Morris Janowitz, Glencoe, Ill: the Free Press of Glencoe, Inc., 1961, p. 17.

The metropolitan area is the dominant form of spatial community in the present society of large and increasing scale. It is also a new form: the wide and variegated pattern of settlement reflects the consequences of changes in the space-time ratio, increase in the surplus, and the extension of networks of interdependence, communication, and control. The changes have far outrun the older models of local government, and the specific form of the generalized norms which provided their legitimation. We harvest the results in a weak and passive governmental response to ongoing change. As our world is transformed these older forms change their meaning—become, in fact, caricatures of themselves. In many cases defenses against any government at all, the multiplying suburbs cause a drift of power upwards to the highest level, the federal bureaucracies.

As problems press and action results, we do see a form of social invention taking place in the metropolis. Special district agencies, government by contract and subcontract, earnings taxes and public corporate enterprise, are ingenious and remarkable stopgaps. They allow us to retain our pieties, while getting on somehow with the job at hand. People get what they want to pay for, within the limits of their inherited folklore and sacred constitutions. Of course, they get many other things in the bargain, some of which they do not want. But the development of large-scale society has been in no respect planned from the present into the future. Nor are we certain of our abilities to do so: the sheer complexity of knowledge required is staggering, while the choice points are really political issues—basic, moral, and not to be solved through scientific argument. For a choice point, in political life, is no simple decision between right and wrong: it is a forced choice between two mutually contradictory values, *both* of which are sacred and precious to someone. Thus it is just as well that the social scientist cannot assume the position of the philosopher-king.

We cannot believe in a wide distribution of power, and

therefore of freedom, and at the same time insist upon a rigorous control of the future. To be sure, this frequently means that we all cooperate in producing something that nobody wants. Such a result may not be simply due to ignorance or clumsiness, however; it may mirror the plural interests of a pluralistic society. The loose system allows some room for variation and innovation (though inplementing them is difficult) ; while it greatly overweights the experiences of the past, it allows for some continuity. Change *is* accomplished; order *is* maintained. There are even unique values in the present system. How else can the polity of a village be reproduced in large-scale society, save in residential municipalities? Furthermore, where else in our society are the segregated, the insulted and injured, as fairly represented as in *their* municipality, the central city? Such results were not planned. "The metropolitan community is continuously improvised; its evolution is organic, not rational; change is crescive, not revolutionary; problems are solved by trial and error rather than by fiat."[8]

Suggested Readings

On the Future Course of the Metropolis

Metropolis 1985, Raymond Vernon, Cambridge: Harvard University Press, 1960. An economist details a broad forecast of the future metropolitan region on the basis of present trends and their economic meaning. He envisages a city which is an enormous connurbation (urban sprawl) with thriving central business districts and enormous areas of downgraded residential housing—"gray areas" as he terms them. Should his projection be accurate, many current policies are somewhat out of kilter with reality.

The Emerging City: Myth and Reality, Scott Greer, New York: Free

[8] *The Emerging City, Myth and Reality*, Scott Greer, New York: The Free Press of Glencoe, Inc., 1962.

Press of Glencoe, Inc., 1962. This approach is kin to that of Vernon but emphasizes the importance of continued increases in social surplus, education, and choice in life-style among metropolitan residents. The consequences for government are then spelled out.

On the Future Polity

The Quest for Community, A Study in the Ethics of Order and Freedom, Robert A. Nisbet, New York: Oxford University Press, 1953. This is a serious and penetrating discussion of the effects of changing social structure on the democratic ethos and the belief in local self-determinism. The growth of the national system is analyzed in relation to the breakdown of the subcommunity at every level.

"Individual Participation in Mass Society." Scott Greer, in Roland Young, editor, Approaches to the Study of Politics, Evanston: Northwestern University Press, 1957. An essay in which the present patterns of social participation, in local community and organization, are described and, on this ground, the assumptions of democratic self-government are examined.

Index

Author's Note: In view of the brevity of this book and the detailed Table of Contents provided, an exhaustive subject index seems redundant. Instead there follow indexes of (*a*) authors to whom reference is made, and (*b*) places named in the text.

a. AUTHORS

Adrian, C, R., 47
Almendinger, V. V., 116, 128
American Academy of Political and Social Sciences, 58

Banfield, E., 65, 76, 78, 79, 81, 128
Bell, W., 14, 41
Bollens, J., 57, 87–88
Bryce, J., 45

Cottrell, F., 22
Cutright, P., 70

Daedelus, 128
Davis, K., 8
Detroit Area Study, 14
Dobriner, W. A., 41, 104
Dreiser, T., 63

Emerson, R. W., 9

Faulkner, W., 9
Fortune, editors of, 22

Galbraith, J. K., 129
Greer, S., 22, 60, 88, 89, 104, 125, 148, 149
Grodzins, M., 128

Hatt, P. K., 42

Hauser, P., 57, 69
Hunter, F., 64

Jacobs, J., 42
Janowitz, M., 42, 67, 68, 70, 146
Jones, V., 58

Kaufman, H., 70, 79, 82, 131
Key, V. O., 72
Kipling, R., 51

Long, N. E., 125
Low, Seth, 46
Lynd, R. and H., 30

Mark Twain, 12
McKenzie, R. D., 121
Moses, L., 136
Mumford, L., 19

Nisbet, R. A., 149

Olmstead, D. W., 67

Park, R. E., 29
Pirenne, H., 21
Plunkitt, G. W., 46, 62

Reichley, J., 70, 81
Reiss, A. J., 42

Riesman, D., 104
Rossi, P. H., 70

Sayre, W. S., 70, 79, 82, 131
Schulze, R. O., 67
Scoble, H., 68
Shevky, E., 14, 41
Sofen, E., 123
Steffens, L., 63
Strauss, A., 54

Theodorson, G. A., 42
Thoreau, H. D., 9
Turner, R., 6, 21

Vernon, R., 136, 141, 148, 149

Wood, R., 87, 102, 104, 115, 116,
    128, 131, 140, 141, 145, 146
Woodbury, C., 58
Whyte, W. F., 70, 81

Young, R., 149

b. PLACES

Alabama, 24
Atlanta, 64

Baltimore, 24
Boston, 70

California, 5, 26
Chicago, 5, 11, 15, 17, 18, 24, 34,
    37, 59, 60, 63, 65, 72, 81, 97–
    102
Cleveland, 65, 120, 122
Cook County Suburbs, 97–102
Culver City (Los Angeles), 86

Dade County, Florida, 54–55
Deerfield (Chicago), 95
Detroit, 13, 86, 121

El Paso-Juarez, 121
England, 8, 10

Europe, 7, 16, 28
Evanston (Chicago), 103

Gary, Indiana, 70, 86
Germany, 24
Great Britain, 24

Hamtramck (Detroit), 86
Houston, 15

Ireland, 24
Italy, 7, 24, 29

Jefferson City, Missouri, 47

Kansas, 13
Kinloch (St. Louis), 86

Las Vegas, 14
Los Angeles, 11, 12, 14, 24, 69,
    77, 86, 129

Memphis, 47
Miami, 120
Miami Beach, 14
Miami Metropolitan Area, 122 ff.
Milwaukee, 11
Minneapolis-St. Paul, 15
Mobile, 47
Moscow, 12

New England, 68
New York City, 3, 5, 8, 13, 19, 24,
    34, 37, 45, 59, 60, 70, 79, 82
New York Metropolitan Area, 52,
    102, 128

Philadelphia, 8, 19, 59, 81
Pittsburgh, 34, 111, 122
Poland, 24, 29

Red Wing, Minnesota, 67
Rome, 6, 8, 10, 12, 24, 111
Russia, 24

San Francisco, 11, 59, 109, 120
Springfield, Illinois, 72
"Stackton" (Gary, Indiana), 70
St. Louis, 15, 24, 47, 58, 65, 72,
    75, 86, 88–90, 94, 96, 120, 122,
    125 ff., 129
St. Louis County, 87, 102, 113, 116

University City (St. Louis), 86,
    103

Upward Ho! (Chicago), 97–99

Valhalla (Chicago), 99–102, 116,
    144
Venice, 8

Washington, D.C., 5, 41
Wichita, Kansas, 13

Ypsilanti, Michigan, 67